Writer/Designer

A Guide to Making Multimodal Projects

Writer/Designer

A Guide to Making Multimodal Projects

Third Edition

Cheryl E. Ball
Wayne State University

Jennifer Sheppard
San Diego State University

Kristin L. Arola
Michigan State University

bedford/st.martin's
Macmillan Learning

Boston | New York

For Bedford/St. Martin's

Vice President: Leasa Burton
Program Director: Stacey Purviance
Program Manager: Laura Arcari
Director of Content Development: Jane Knetzger
Associate Editor: Suzanne H Chouljian
Editorial Assistant: Annie Campbell
Director of Media Editorial: Adam Whitehurst
Marketing Manager: Vivian Garcia
Senior Director, Content Management Enhancement: Tracey Kuehn
Senior Managing Editor: Michael Granger
Senior Manager of Publishing Services: Andrea Cava
Senior Content Project Manager: Lidia MacDonald-Carr
Senior Workflow Project Manager: Lisa McDowell
Production Supervisor: Robin Besofsky
Director of Design, Content Management: Diana Blume
Interior Design: Claire Seng-Niemoeller
Cover Design: William Boardman
Director of Rights and Permissions: Hilary Newman
Text Permissions Researcher: Maisie Howell
Photo Researcher: Krystyna Borgen, Lumina Datamatics, Inc.
Director of Digital Production: Keri deManigold
Media Project Manager: Elizabeth Dziubela
Project Management: Lumina Datamatics, Inc.
Senior Project Manager: Aravinda Doss, Lumina Datamatics, Inc.
Editorial Services: Lumina Datamatics, Inc.
Composition: Lumina Datamatics, Inc.
Printing and Binding: R.R. Donnelley

Library of Congress Control Number: 2021930832
ISBN 978-1-319-24505-4

Printed in China.
1   2   3   4   5   6   26   25   24   23   22   21

Acknowledgments

Acknowledgments and copyrights appear on the same page as the text and art selections they cover; these acknowledgments and copyrights constitute an extension of the copyright page.

For information, write: Bedford/St. Martin's, 75 Arlington Street, Boston, MA 02116

Preface for Instructors

We know that creating multimodal projects and assignments can seem daunting and bring up a lot of questions for both students and instructors. What's the best way to get students started with a multimodal project? Is it necessary to learn a lot of new technologies? How do you introduce multimodal activities into the writing classroom, even if the final project is text-based? How do you assess multimodal work? In this third edition of *Writer/Designer*, we aim to help you answer these questions and more, making multimodal composing strategies and projects even more accessible and relatable to you and your students. We know how to help you through it because we've been there—throughout the book, you'll be learning from the successes, mistakes, and experiences we've had teaching, supervising, and creating multimodal work in classes ranging from first-year writing to advanced media courses.

The title of this book, *Writer/Designer: A Guide to Making Multimodal Projects*, reflects our belief that writing and designing always work together. Whether authors are working with words, images, sound, or movement, decisions about what content says and how it looks and functions are necessarily entwined, even when we don't pay conscious attention to their relationship. We want our students to always be aware of how writing and designing work together, to think of themselves as equal parts writers and designers. Both design and content influence how audiences respond to a text's message, so developing familiarity with design concepts and practices as well as textual and rhetorical composition is critical for successful communication. This book helps students to develop these skills together, providing them with a rhetorical toolkit for making purposeful, relevant, and persuasive choices in their writing and designing.

The concepts of design and process that we introduce in this book provide a foundation for any composition course and a guide for any instructor looking to incorporate multimodality, no matter your experience or expertise with media or technologies.

For this third edition, we listened to feedback from composition instructors—program administrators, professors, graduate students, and part-time faculty—teaching in two-year schools and four-year schools, online courses and cinder-block-walled classrooms, to make *Writer/Designer* even more flexible and accommodating to different course objectives and instructors' varying levels of comfort with teaching multimodality. Revised Touchpoint activities showcase ideas for multimodal practice through learning key writing and design concepts, and these can be used independently as in-class work. Detailed Write/Design! assignments are designed to lend you support and guidance, and the Write/Design! options in the chapter-ending assignments present ways to incorporate multimodality into core writing assignments, such as literacy narratives and rhetorical analyses.

Through highlighting new student examples, foregrounding rhetoric, and updating examples to be representative of the times in which we currently live, the third edition of *Writer/Designer* illustrates how and why multimodality can amplify underrepresented voices and help to enact change. We also continue with our commitment to support instructors' and students' teaching and learning of the multimodal composing process in creative and engaging ways.

Although the focus of *Writer/Designer* is on helping students develop compositional and rhetorical strategies, we also provide explanations of multimodality's value that will be of use to instructors who need to make the case that facility with diverse literacies and modalities will strengthen students' rhetorical and communicative skills. The book's accompanying Instructor's Manual provides clear, accessible guidance for teaching multimodal composition that will help ambassadors discuss multimodal pedagogy with writing program administrators, department heads, colleagues, and teaching assistants.

Multimodality, Genres, and Life

Multimodal texts have become an essential part of communication in nearly every arena of contemporary culture. The widespread use of design software, online technologies, and other digital media has increased opportunities to convey information and has also changed the expectations of readers. We wrote this book specifically to help authors learn how to make conscious multimodal choices in the texts they create, no matter what mode, medium, or rhetorical situation they are working in. With the guidance and activities we've provided in *Writer/Designer*, authors—your students—will be better prepared for the complex rhetorical challenges they face as students and future professionals.

We designed this book to support the integration of multimodal projects into classrooms through both short-term and semester-long projects. The book offers flexible, accessible strategies for composing with multiple modes of communication, including detailed explanations of what multimodality means, definitions and examples of key design concepts, rationales for why multi-modality matters, and in-depth support for composing multimodal projects within a variety of contexts and technologies. The chapters use a mix of student-produced and real-world projects to illustrate the rhetorical choices and strategies discussed.

Like the second edition, this third edition is designed to lead authors through a chronological process in analyzing, planning, and designing multimodal texts in Part One and to apply specific strategies and tools from the Toolkit in Part Two, according to the affordances and needs of their particular projects and processes. New marginal callouts to the Write/Design Toolkit link concepts throughout Part One to more in-depth guidance and helpful tools in Part Two. The assignments we've included can support authors in creating their own projects in any genre or situation. Our original inspiration for the book came from talking with colleagues in fields as diverse as business, political science, and geology about the kinds of multimodal texts they asked their students to produce, and about how those processes could be supported using the rhetorical methods we teach within our own writing classes. *Writer/Designer* is meant to be easy to use in any number of courses across disciplines, either on its own or bundled with your favorite textbook or handbook. The Instructor's Manual includes sample syllabi to demonstrate how *Writer/Designer* can be used in a variety of courses, as well as tips and strategies for using the activities in your in-person or online course.

Grounded in Theory, Supported in Practice

This book is grounded in our own praxes, pedagogies, and theoretical leanings. As friends in graduate school in the early 2000s, we were immersed in the New London Group's (NLG) pedagogy of multiliteracies when it was used by our writing program faculty to reimagine the first-year writing course we all taught. The NLG—a group of literacy scholars from across the globe—make the case that multimodal pedagogies more richly prepare students for the diverse rhetorical and communicative practices they need to succeed as students, as professionals, and as citizens in the twenty-first century.

As composition instructors, rather than concentrating exclusively on written text, we were introduced to a model of composition instruction that focused on integrating written, oral, and visual communication. This curriculum helped students learn to craft texts in a variety of modes and genres to best meet their diverse rhetorical needs.

In the years since our first experiences in that multimodal classroom, we've gone on to specialize in different areas of rhetoric and writing studies, but the theory and pedagogy of what we experienced in those early days continue to influence our work today. Cheryl's work as editor of the journal *Kairos* helps the field of writing studies rethink how scholarship about digital writing can be modeled in digital, multimodal forms; Jenny regularly teaches courses in professional communication and digital, visual, and popular culture rhetorics, and she publishes on the intersection of theory and practice in digital writing, multimodal composing, professional communication, and pedagogy; and Kristin's work brings together composition theory, digital rhetoric, and American Indian rhetorics so as to understand digital composing practices within larger social and cultural contexts. As we've developed and refined syllabi in a variety of courses, created our own multimodal projects, and mentored authors through their composition processes, we've discovered a series of best practices, backed up by theory, that we want to share with you. This book benefits from our collective experiences and builds from many of the assignments and syllabi we've designed, as well as from the editorial process Cheryl uses in *Kairos*. You can see some of these syllabi and other curricular materials in the Instructor's Manual.

The examples and processes discussed in this book draw from both classroom and real-world texts to help students see how multimodality works in a variety of contexts and genres. We provide tools for critically analyzing available resources, as well as for understanding how different modes can be brought together in creative and complex ways to convey new meanings across multiple, new situations. Research in rhetorical genre studies suggests that this method of recursive analysis and production, specifically done within genres that are found in everyday life, helps authors learn how to write in multiple situations. The Instructor's Manual offers an annotated bibliography that covers issues of rhetorical genre studies, multiliteracies, multimodal composition, and more.

Features of the Book

- **A process-focused approach** introduces and illustrates key stages of multimodal composition while establishing clear connections to the writing process and to the practices students will actually use in creating their projects.

- **A central emphasis on design** introduces and illustrates foundational concepts of design—*contrast, organization, alignment, proximity*, and more—to provide students the tools they need to develop multimodal texts.

- **Write/Design! assignments** in every Part One chapter help students dig into chapter concepts and scaffold students' development of larger-scale projects. They ask students to complete assignments such as a genre conventions analysis for their chosen project, a proposal for developing and delivering their multimodal projects, and a report on the final project or draft. **Write/Design! options** offer assignment options in classes where asking students to complete a large-scale, semester-long project may not be desirable. They ask students to complete activities such as a multimodal literacy narrative, rhetorical analysis of several multimodal texts of their choosing, and a genre analysis of visual arguments.

- **Touchpoint** activities throughout each chapter prepare students to apply multimodal concepts from the book to small-stakes practice—either sample multimedia texts and scenarios (in Part One) or their own projects (in Part Two). Touchpoint activities teach students about practices such as examining modal affordances, analyzing project designs, learning about fair use and different kinds of Creative Commons licenses, developing practices for successful collaboration, and creating drafts of their projects through rapid prototyping techniques.

- **Case Studies** highlight and analyze actual examples of multimodal texts, sourced from student writer/designers and professional publications. In Case Studies, we provide in-depth analyses of an author's composing processes that correspond to the stage of writing/designing outlined in that chapter. Case Studies also showcase how the design vocabulary or concepts we present in each chapter are put into practice in the design process. Example texts from Case Studies include a deep dive into the modal affordances of a COVID-19 impact map, a rhetorical and design analysis of a college website, and a student team's pitch for an interactive museum app.

Whether you are new to teaching multimodal projects or someone who has lots of experience, we designed this book to give your students a strong foundation in the concepts and practices of multimodal composing. You'll also find the additional materials in the Instructor's Manual helpful. In it, we've compiled more assignments, syllabi, and supporting content to provide further ideas on integrating multimodality into your writing classes.

New to This Edition

From the outset, *Writer/Designer* was meant to be an attractive, brief, accessible, and highly readable guide to multimodal composition. While the third edition remains committed to these goals, it also seeks to highlight the unique position that multimodal composition occupies in times of fake news and sociopolitical echo chambers. Multimodal texts have long been used to share information and raise awareness of important issues. This third edition seeks to emphasize the ways in which authors can write/design multimodal texts in ways that amplify historically marginalized voices to bring about social change. With new, diverse examples, more detailed stand-alone activities for in the classroom and out, and updated design coverage, *Writer/Designer* is now more flexible, inclusive, and useful for student writer/designers.

- **More diverse, inclusive examples and images** highlight new perspectives and the creative ways in which multimodal composition can amplify historically marginalized voices. Selections in the third edition span a variety of real-world write/design situations meant to raise awareness for social justice issues, including the Black Lives Matter movement, the Dakota Access Pipeline, LGBTQ+ representation, struggles faced by those with disabilities and chronic illness, and more.

- **More student examples** showcase multimodal texts created by actual students in relatable rhetorical situations. While *Writer/Designer* emphasizes the value and impact that writer/designers' compositions will have in the real world, the third edition packs in even more creative student models to guide authors as they write/design throughout their academic careers.

- **New Case Studies** analyze more relevant and realistic examples of rhetorical situations, design choices, technological affordances, and the multimodal design process. New examples include a deep dive into a COVID-19 impact map in Chapter 1, and an analysis of Chemeketa Community College's website in Chapter 2.

- **New Write/Design Toolkit marginal callouts** connect foundational concepts covered in Part One to relevant best practices included in Part Two: The Write/Design Toolkit. These marginal callouts encourage students to start thinking about important considerations—like searching for and documenting sources, collaborating with others, technological affordances, and preparing for the multimodal afterlife—early on in the design process.

Acknowledgments

This book would never have been possible without the guidance and support of the people we worked with over the years at Bedford/St. Martin's. For their early inspiration for this book, we'd like to thank Joan Feinberg and Denise Wydra. We would also like to thank Leasa Burton, Vice President of Macmillan Learning Humanities Editorial; Stacey Purviance, Program Director for English; and Laura Arcari, Senior Program Manager for English. Suzy Chouljian proved her professional mettle in providing us with clear guidance and excellent revision suggestions on this third edition, and her bright spirit during the tough year of 2020 helped us complete our tasks with grace. Thank you to Lucy Johnson, University of Wisconsin–Eau Claire, for tackling the revision of earlier editions of the Instructor's Manual.

We'd also like to recognize the many other people at Bedford who contributed to this book: Lidia MacDonald-Carr, Senior Content Project Manager, and Aravinda Doss, Senior Project Manager, for their patience and attention to detail; Michael Van Atta, copyeditor; William Boardman, Cover Designer; Vivian Garcia, Marketing Manager, for working to get the word out about the book; Hilary Newman, Director of Rights and Permissions, and Krystyna Borgen, Photo Researcher; and May Hasso, indexer, for her careful attention to themes and subjects. Thank you, thank you, thank you.

Thanks are also due to the following reviewers and consultants, for their invaluable guidance and feedback throughout this revision: Ashley Beardsley, The University of Oklahoma; Amanda Bemer, Southwest Minnesota State University; Lee Skallerup Bessette, Georgetown University; Collin Bjork, Massey University; Jillian Boger, University of Rhode Island; Emily Brooks; Elizabeth Burrows, Auburn University at Montgomery; Lauren E. Cagle, University of Kentucky; Christopher Castillo, University of Wisconsin–Madison; Pamela Chisum; Jenae Cohn; Richard Colby, University of Denver; Sydney Darby, Chemeketa Community College; Scott Lloyd DeWitt, The Ohio State University; Shane Empie; Harley Ferris, The University of Findlay; Wilfredo Flores, Michigan State University; Crystal N. Fodrey, Moravian College; Bre Garrett, University of West Florida; Risa Gorelick-Ollom, New Jersey Institute of Technology; Dale Grauman; Jennifer Hart, Wayne State University; Cynthia Haynes, Clemson University; Carley Johanson; Fred Johnson, Whitworth University; Lucy Johnson, University of Wisconsin–Eau Claire; Elizabeth L. Jones, University of Nevada, Reno; Heather Jordan, Bowling Green State University, Main Campus; Roni Joyner, Howard University; Matthew Kim, Eagle Hill School; Dundee Lackey, Texas Woman's University; Ana Cortes Lagos, Syracuse University; Amanda Licastro, University of Pennsylvania; Amy Locklear, Auburn University at Montgomery; Joy McMurrin, Dixie State University; Sierra Mendez, The University of Texas at Austin; Cara Marta Messina; Lorri Mon; Elizabeth Monske, Northern Michigan University; Kristen Moore, University at Buffalo; Jill Morris, Frostburg State University; Paul Muhlhauser, McDaniel College; Scott Pennington; Margaret Price, The Ohio State University; Jessica Rajko, Wayne State University; Scott Reed, Georgia Gwinnett College; Lynn Reid, Fairleigh Dickinson University College at Florham; Joy Santee; Wendi Sierra, Texas Christian University; Tamara Tate; Todd Taylor, The University of North Carolina at Chapel Hill; Crystal VanKooten, Oakland University; Lydia Wilkes, Idaho State University; and George Williams, University of Georgia. Their insights helped us to focus our approach and to keep the needs of a diverse instructor and student population in mind as we wrote.

We'd like to say a special thanks to the people in our immediate lives who have supported our work on this project. We are grateful to our many students, colleagues, and friends who allowed us to use examples of their work to help others learn. These samples would not have been possible without their graciousness.

Cheryl would like to thank Jenny and Kristin for, yet still, putting up with her. She would also like to thank the many colleagues, known and new, who have brought forward their love of Writer/Designer on social media platforms so that we can know our work has been of use to folks in the field.

Jenny would like to extend her thanks to her partner, Kathryn, who graciously took on extra childcare and household duties while she worked on the book. Her overall support and willingness to talk through ideas were instrumental in the project's completion. Jenny would also like to thank Jen Almjeld,

Cody Archer, Edgar Barrantes, Edreanne "Anna" Calaycay, Hannah Willis Castellanos, Iris Xinyue Chen, Paul Jensen, Eirein Gaile Harn, Phillip Johnson, Alicía Leon, Joyce Melendez, Cory Moore, Erica Mosley, Sarah Tanori, Alejandra Villavicencio, and Angela Wilson for their permission to reproduce several of the examples used in the book, as well as the many students with whom she has worked over the years. She has learned an immeasurable amount about multimodal composing from their efforts and experiences.

Kristin would like to thank all of the amazing students and colleagues she's had the privilege of learning from over the years. She stands on the shoulders of many, but the pedagogical prowess of Patricia Ericsson, Lucy Johnson, Amy Petersilie, and Everardo Cuevas greatly shapes how she thinks about multi-modal composing. She sends a huge thanks to current and past students who share their work with you in this book—Huizi Li, Nicole Schmidt, Courteney Dowd, Ariel Popp, Nicholas Winters, Elyse Canfield, Hailey Deyo, Kaylee Mullen, Amelia Turkette, Nicole Adams, Oliviah Brown, and Logan Bry. Thanks also to the artists who share their work here (Dylan Miner and Adam Arola), and who help us imagine better worlds and dance through what we've got. And finally, *chi miigwech* to Jeff for shouldering extra childcare and household labor (during a pandemic, no less!) so that this edition could be completed.

Bedford/St. Martin's puts you first

From day one, our goal has been simple: to provide inspiring resources that are grounded in best practices for teaching reading and writing. For more than 40 years, Bedford/St. Martin's has partnered with the field, listening to teachers, scholars, and students about the support writers need. No matter the moment or teaching context, we are committed to helping every writing instructor make the most of our resources—resources designed to engage every student.

How can we help *you*?

- Our editors can align our resources to your outcomes through correlation and transition guides for your syllabus. Just ask us.
- Our sales representatives specialize in helping you find the right materials to support your course goals.
- Our learning solutions and product specialists help you make the most of the digital resources you choose for your course.
- Our *Bits* blog on the Bedford/St. Martin's English Community (**community.macmillan.com**) publishes fresh teaching ideas regularly. You'll also find easily downloadable professional resources and links to author webinars on our community site.

Contact your Bedford/St. Martin's sales representative or visit **macmillanlearning.com** to learn more.

Digital and Print Options for *Writer/Designer*

Choose the format that works best for your course, and ask about our packaging options that offer savings for students.

Digital

- *Achieve for Writer's Help*. Achieve puts student writing at the center of your course and keeps revision at the core, with a dedicated composition space that guides students through drafting, peer review, plagiarism prevention, reflection, and revision. Developed to support best practices in commenting on student drafts, Achieve is a flexible, integrated suite of tools for designing and facilitating writing assignments, paired with actionable insights that make students' progress toward outcomes clear and measurable. With trusted content from the widely used Hacker or Lunsford handbooks, *Writer's Help* takes students through first-year writing and beyond. For details, visit **macmillanlearning.com/college/us /achieve/english**.

- *Popular e-book formats.* For details about our e-book partners, visit **macmillanlearning.com/ebooks**.

- *Inclusive Access.* Enable every student to receive their course materials through your LMS on the first day of class. Macmillan Learning's Inclusive Access program is the easiest, most affordable way to ensure all students have access to quality educational resources. Find out more at **macmillanlearning.com/inclusiveaccess**.

Print

- *Spiral-bound.* To order the spiral-bound edition, use ISBN 978-1-319-24505-4.

Your Course, Your Way

No two writing programs or classrooms are exactly alike. Our Curriculum Solutions team works with you to design custom options that provide the resources your students need. (Options below require enrollment minimums.)

- *ForeWords for English.* Customize any print resource to fit the focus of your course or program by choosing from a range of prepared topics, such as Sentence Guides for Academic Writers.

- *Macmillan Author Program (MAP).* Add excerpts or package acclaimed works from Macmillan's trade imprints to connect students with prominent authors and public conversations. A list of popular examples or academic themes is available upon request.

- *Mix and Match.* With our simplest solution, you can add up to 50 pages of curated content to your Bedford/St. Martin's text. Contact your sales representative for additional details.

Instructor Resources

You have a lot to do in your course. We want to make it easy for you to find the support you need—and to get it quickly.

The *Instructor's Manual for Writer/Designer* is available as a PDF that can be downloaded from **macmillanlearning.com**. In addition to chapter overviews and teaching tips for in-person and online classes, the Instructor's Manual includes sample syllabi, correlations to the Council of Writing Program Administrators' Outcomes Statement, and classroom activities.

Contents

4   How Do You Start a Multimodal Project?   84

5   How Do You Design and Revise with Multiple Audiences?   109

PART TWO   The Write/Design Toolkit

6 Working with Multimodal Assets and Sources   145

Introduction for Students

such a lot about digital texts. We'll give you pointers for multimodal texts, too. Also, this isn't a how-to book about specific technologies or software applications. We'll give you guidance on how to think through the who, what, why, when, and how

Although the three of us are trained as writing teachers, we have always been interested in multimodal communication. Don't get us wrong; we love words, and we love helping people learn how to craft them. However, we also believe that elements beyond words can be just as effective—or more so!—in conveying a message. Our goal in this book is to help you take advantage of every possibility that's out there—not just words but also sound, images, movement, and more—so you can create communications that perfectly meet your goals, your situation, and the needs of your audience.

We often ask our students to create texts of all kinds, and we decided to write this book as a way to support writers in that complex and sometimes messy process. As writers, designers, and communicators who for many years have worked on creating interactive digital projects, video presentations, websites, social networking profiles, new media journals, online courses, and more, we are interested in conveying information and ideas using the most appropriate means and media at our disposal. Through this book, you'll learn from the successes we've had and the mistakes we've made as teachers and authors.

Notice we just said "authors" here, but elsewhere in this book we'll refer to the people who produce content as "designers," "writers," and "communicators." You might be saying that writers don't design, or that communicators don't write. We don't believe that's true (and that's why we called this book *Writer/ Designer*). Using a multimodal approach to reading or composing a text, you'll start to recognize that *all* writing is designed, even if it doesn't look like much thought was put into those one-inch margins. The converse is usually true as well, in that most designs involve some kind of writing. We believe that communication comes in many forms and that it is all created with some deliberate attention to writing and design. It may not be a kind of writing that you recognize or that you think would "count" as acceptable writing in a professional setting, such as school or work, but as this book will show you, even something as seemingly simple as a text message can be carefully written and designed.

At this point in your life, you've likely come to realize that good writing doesn't just happen. You're probably familiar with the idea that writing is a process, with various stages required to get to a final product. Similarly, good multimodal projects don't just happen—they involve planning, researching, drafting, and revising. Although these stages may look a little different for each writer and each project, being able to draw on this basic process can help you create texts that will be complete and persuasive to your intended audience. This book will help you hone a composing process that works for you, no matter what kind of project you are creating.

Just as important, this book will provide you with a toolkit for analyzing and creating texts in many modes and for many different audiences. Although we'll talk a lot about digital texts, we'll provide ideas for nondigital texts, too. Also, this isn't a how-to book about specific technologies or software applications. We'll give you guidance on how to think through the *who*, *what*, *why*, and *how* of your projects so that you can use whichever communication mode, genre, or technology will best suit your audience and purpose. You'll find that this approach is more beneficial in the long run because you'll be able to apply these practices to whatever new technology emerges next.

Features of the Book and How to Use Them

We spent a lot of time thinking about how to design this book to support the variety of projects you might take on. We've worked to provide clear explanations and lots of examples, particularly in the Case Studies, to help illustrate the concepts and practices we talk about. We have included short Touchpoint activities throughout each chapter so that you can get some quick experience putting concepts into practice. We've also included longer Write/Design! assignments (with options) in each chapter in Part One to guide you through the steps of creating larger-scale projects. We have used many of these activities and assignments with our own students to help them develop ideas, design projects, and communicate through multiple modes.

Above all, as you use this book, we want you to keep in mind that creating multimodal projects can be a lot of fun. Yes, there are bound to be frustrations along the way as you work through the many possibilities, but your communication options are no longer limited to typing words in a twelve-point font on an 8.5" × 11" piece of paper. We invite you to dive in, experiment, and see what opportunities you have to convey your ideas, arguments, and information.

Writer/Designer

A Guide to Making Multimodal Projects

PART ONE

The Multimodal Process

What Are Multimodal Projects?

Academic essays, biology posters, PowerPoint presentations, Tweets, TikTok videos . . . what do all these texts have in common? They are all **multimodal**.

The word *multimodal* is a mash-up of *multiple* and *mode*. A **mode** is a way of communicating, such as the words we're using to explain our ideas in this paragraph or the images we use throughout this book to illustrate various concepts. Multimodal describes how we combine multiple different ways of communicating in everyday life.

For instance, many Instagram posts are multimodal. They usually combine photos or short videos of beautiful, funny, or everyday experiences with short descriptions and hashtags to create a text that uses visuals, language, and sometimes sound—*multiple modes*.

You might be saying to yourself, "Wait, is an Instagram post really a text?" Yes. **Text** traditionally means written words. But because we want to talk about not just words, but the visuals, sounds, and movement that make up multimedia, we use the term *text* to refer to a piece of communication as a whole. A text can be anything from a photo to a concert tee shirt to a news article to a dance performance (**Fig. 1.4**).

Figures 1.1 to **1.4** all depict multimodal texts:

Figure 1.1 An Instagram Post

Jennifer Sheppard

Figure 1.2 A Website

Erica Mosley

RWS 414

Dr. Sheppard

20 March 2018

How Does This Image Personify the Phrase 'Representation Matters'?

Accurate and positive representation of black women in media has been an uphill battle, which is why the unveiling of Amy Sherald's "Michelle LaVaughn Robinson Obama" in the Smithsonian Portrait Gallery in Washington, D.C. is such an iconic moment in history. However, the artifact up for analysis in this essay is not the portrait, but this photo (on the left) of it. This photo is powerful because Parker's facial expression symbolizes how its primary audience, black women, likely feel about the current and long overdue representation of African American women in art and media. Despite her innocent oblivion to it, Parker's reaction makes a powerful rhetorical statement to African American women, and women all over the country: representation matters. This essay will explore how Parker personifies the phrase "representation matters" using visual rhetoric and photo analysis strategies.

Figure 1- Photo captured by Mhari Shaw of four-year-old Parker looking up awe-struck at Michelle Obama's portrait in the Smithsonian Portrait Gallery.

Figure 1.3 Student Paper

Courtesy of Erica Mosley; photo: Mhari Shaw/NPR

Figure 1.4 A Performance

Timothy J. Carroll; https://www.flickr.com/photos/tjc/5763847134

What Is Multimodal Composing?

Writers choose modes of communication for every text they create. For example, the author of a YouTube video decides what content to show, if they want to include text on-screen or in the description, and what dialogue or music they want to use. Sometimes these choices are unconscious, like when an author uses Microsoft Word's default typeface and margins when writing a paper for class. Sometimes those choices are made explicitly by an author, and that's when **design** becomes purposeful. To produce a successful text, writer/designers must be able to consciously use different modes both alone and in combination to communicate their ideas to others.

A text does not have to include bright colors or interesting videos to be multimodal (although it can). Even a research paper, which consists mostly of words, is a multimodal text. Let's take **Figure 1.3** as an example. It might seem that an audience could understand this text's argument just by reading the written words. However, to understand the full message being communicated in the text, the audience has to make sense of other elements as well. They must also look at the images and read the caption that explains what the image contains. Even the font choice is an important but often subtle visual signal to the audience. The format of the text—a single column of black printed words on a white background; the header with name, page number, and course information—also tells the audience something important: This text is probably an academic work of some kind. Knowing what kind of text it is (its genre) will influence the way the audience reads it.

Why Should Multimodal Composing Matter to You?

Multimodal projects are fun! But they're not *just* fun. They're useful and flexible and timely—just as writing is—while also doing double or triple the communicative work of writing due to the multiple layers of meaning that the modes of communication carry. They provide more ways to communicate your message, allowing you to reach and persuade larger audiences.

Take, for example, **Figure 1.5**. Artist Katherine Young was unhappy with the way girls' magazines portrayed their needs and goals in a way that only emphasized fashion and friends. The original cover of *Girls' Life* uses color, font size, and capitalization to draw readers' attention to the magazine's features, all related to appearance or relationships: fashion, kisses, "dream" hair, and "Wake up pretty!" An arrow and curved line just under the title connects the cover model with what the magazine deems valuable: her style. Young redesigned this magazine cover to emphasize girls' needs and goals involving career, health,

Figure 1.5 The Original *Girls' Life* Cover (left) and Young's Redesign (right)

and community. By reusing an existing design for the teen magazine genre and making intentional choices for text, font, color, image, and layout, Young made a multimodal feminist statement—without needing to explicitly state the issue or her argument.

In the world, in your everyday life, texts are never monomodal, never *just* written, but are always designed with multiple media, modes of communication, and methods of distribution in mind. Learning how to analyze and compose multimodal texts prepares you for this more diverse kind of writing—the kind you will use every day of your life. Whether you work from home, in a large corporation, in a small nonprofit organization, or in some other professional or personal setting, you *will* need to write. And writing in the twenty-first century is always multimodal.

This whole book is about the *what* and *how* of multimodal composition, but the *why* is the motivation for it. We draw inspiration from a group of multimodal communication scholars (called the New London Group) who explain the *why* this way: Multimodal composition allows us to become **makers of our social futures**. That sounds exciting, doesn't it? But what exactly does it mean? By learning to compose multimodal texts instead of rehashing the limited use of written essays, writer/designers can use a broader toolkit to communicate in more globally aware, digitally driven, socially just, and accessible ways, making our society a better place. The magazine cover redesign in **Figure 1.5** is a great example of using multimodality to (re)make our social futures. Similarly, consider the powerful role publications like *Teen Vogue* have played in redefining norms and expectations for young adults—focusing on issues of social justice and representing a range of bodies on their covers and in their pages.

Research-based writing typical of academic essays is important, but it's only one part of learning how to write. Authors need to be flexible and draw on any possible way to communicate that might be effective. Aristotle argued that rhetoric, a concept we will explore in Chapter 2, is the skill of leveraging "all available means of persuasion." By this, he meant that people who want to convince others to think or act in a particular way should consider all the strategies at their disposal rather than just reusing methods that have worked in the past. While Aristotle didn't have access to the multimodal possibilities we have today, the fundamental goals of writing and designing are the same:

- To think critically about the kinds of communication that are needed in any given situation.
- To choose sources and assets that will help create a persuasive and effective text.

- To work within and fulfill your audience's expectations, needs, and goals.
- To create clear, informed, and persuasive texts.
- To create change or encourage positive action through a text.

While these aims for multimodality might seem grandiose if you're just learning how to design a text, they can be implemented in even the smallest of ways. Using an image, for example, can speak volumes towards a designer's goal of being globally, ethically, and accessibly aware through multimodality. There are more than seven billion people in the world and thousands of languages. Writing and designing through multimodality can not only help us make more persuasive cases but can also help us to be more mindful and inclusive in how we represent or collaborate with those who are not exactly like us.

Multimodal texts can be used ethically to promote social and racial justice. For instance, the photograph in **Figure 1.6** presents an unarmed, peaceful protester for Black Lives Matter, Leisha Evans, facing a wall of heavily armed riot police. She stands calmly resolute (we'll talk about the gestural and spatial modes later in this chapter), with hands peacefully outstretched and eyes looking forward towards the violent action about to befall her. As a statement meant

Figure 1.6 Using Images for Social Justice
Jonathan Bachman/Reuters/Newscom

to highlight police violence against Black people, this image is a powerful multimodal text that globally amplified the Movement for Black Lives when the photo went viral.

While a big focus of this book is developing practices to write/design your own multimodal texts, we also want to help you develop strategies for being critical of what others say through these means. We encourage you to think carefully about how such texts are made and how they make meaning so that you can (1) listen to and appreciate the perspective of others, (2) be conscious of how texts are attempting to influence you, and (3) learn how to make your own multimodal arguments to achieve your rhetorical goals and purposes. This book helps you do that, whether you're a student, a teacher, an entrepreneur, a parent, a TikTok fanatic, or all of the above.

All the examples used in this book are meant to provoke discussion as to how texts work through the media and modes they use. We have included a number of multimodal texts composed by our own students to illustrate just how doable this work is for readers like you. Every text is designed for an audience, and the choices made by writer/designers are a big part of whether they are effective or not. There may be examples in this book that you don't connect with, but we've selected a variety to help illustrate lots of multimodal possibilities.

Writing/Designing as a Process

Whenever an author begins writing a text, it is always a **process**, even if that process has become so implicit through practice that the author no longer recognizes the multiple steps they may take to complete a text. They begin from scratch, thinking about what they need to say, who they need to say it to, and how they will communicate it. (This part of the writing process is called *analyzing the rhetorical situation*, which we will discuss in Chapter 2.) No matter the modality, this process of thinking through what and how to communicate one's message is roughly the same.

The Typical Writing Process

Writing a research paper doesn't begin with the moment of inscription—putting words on a page. A lot of thinking, talking, brainstorming, and research needs to be done before a topic can even be settled on. But once an author begins writing a paper, it will probably go through multiple rounds of writing and revision, particularly if it is a high-stakes project like a research paper, thesis, or business report. Drafting might involve preliminary research on the audience, topic, genre, and delivery method required (such as types of sources or citation systems needed).

Any necessary revisions require the author to revisit the drafting and formatting stages before presenting the final text to the audience. This writing process is called *recursive* because writers repeat the same cycle as they work to improve their text through interacting with audiences at several parts of the process, getting feedback from sample audiences or stakeholders, and revising—this is a typical process enacted in writing classes. Bringing your attention to the composing process is important because it allows us to break down projects into manageable steps, and it encourages us to be more attentive to what we are trying to communicate and to whom.

> **Write/Design Toolkit**
>
> For more on citing assets, see "Citing Assets and Sources" on page 158.

For instance, **Figure 1.3** (p. 4) shows the front page of a student's rhetorical analysis paper. The writer began by finding the image she wanted to analyze, in this case a photo of a little girl staring in awe at the recently unveiled official portrait of former First Lady Michelle Obama. Then, referring to readings the writer had done in class on how to evaluate visual elements such as color, gaze, and lighting, she began to take notes on the photo and to organize her thoughts for the paper. She sought feedback from her classmates and instructor on her ideas, began revising her text, and finished by working more closely to format the paper with the correct spacing, grammar, punctuation, citation styles, and so on.

The Multimodal Composing Process

When we write texts that are more overtly multimodal than a research paper, we use the same recursive process: different levels of brainstorming, researching, drafting, and revising until we need only to polish the final text. Just as authors choose from available words and genres to create their new texts, designers choose from new and existing examples and assets, working recursively to create a new multimodal text suitable for a new audience. **Figure 1.7** shows sketches (left) and a screenshot (right) from a student's video project. The video analyzes ideological messages in children's stories and how these messages are crafted. The project began with research by looking closely at lots of sample children's books and taking notes on what she saw. The student drew sketches as she was drafting her own children's story to illustrate central themes of self-acceptance. This drafting step was critical in the multimodal

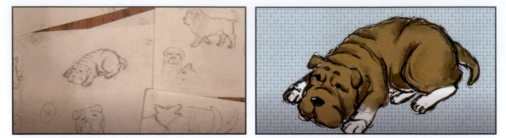

Figure 1.7 A Screenshot and Sketches from a Student Video Analyzing Ideological Themes in Children's Stories

Xinyue (Iris) Chen

composing process as she worked to evoke just the right expressions from her audience before finalizing her full-color drawings, placing them into the video, and adding dialogue and music.

During the design process, multimodal texts may take several different forms. Although some people assume multimodal texts always have to be digital, that's not actually true. A multimodal text may be designed using digital methods (such as a word processor or a video editing application), a mixture of digital and analog methods (such as note cards to draft a PowerPoint presentation or the sketches shown in **Fig. 1.7**), or may be totally analog (such as a pen-and-ink drawing or collage). All these design decisions are based on what the writer/designer needs during the drafting and feedback process and what modes and media will suit the intended audience. We focus on the process of multimodal composing in this book because multimodal texts often require different steps than writing a paper.

For example, when making a video, it's easier to revise based on initial feedback from a storyboard than from a more polished video recording.

Touchpoints

Touchpoints are important to the design process for multimodal projects because they are how designers pinpoint, assess, reflect, and redesign all the different steps in a situation or text as the potential audience will encounter it. The term *touchpoint* comes from the discipline of design, where it refers to real or ephemeral points of interaction between stakeholders (users, service providers, etc.) in a designed experience. Points of interaction vary depending on the kind of experience designers are working with.

Write/Design Toolkit

See "Prototyping for Static Texts" on page 180, "Designing Drafts of Dynamic Texts" on page 184, and "Composing Timeline-Based Drafts" on page 188 for more on the composing process.

For example, one kind of experience might be a tourist using an interactive map at a museum on their phone. As you can see in the screenshot in **Figure 1.8**, touchpoints in that experience could include an app store entry with information on downloading the map, the user's phone connectivity source (wireless data or Wi-Fi) as they navigate the museum, the map interface and how they can interact with it, physical signs in the museum pointing to more detailed exhibit content accessible on the app, the way directions are stored (offline or online only) as they begin their trek, and so on. Hundreds of touchpoints are possible in a single experience, and touchpoints ensure that designers understand the full scope of work they need to create to effectively reach their audience and fulfill a particular need.

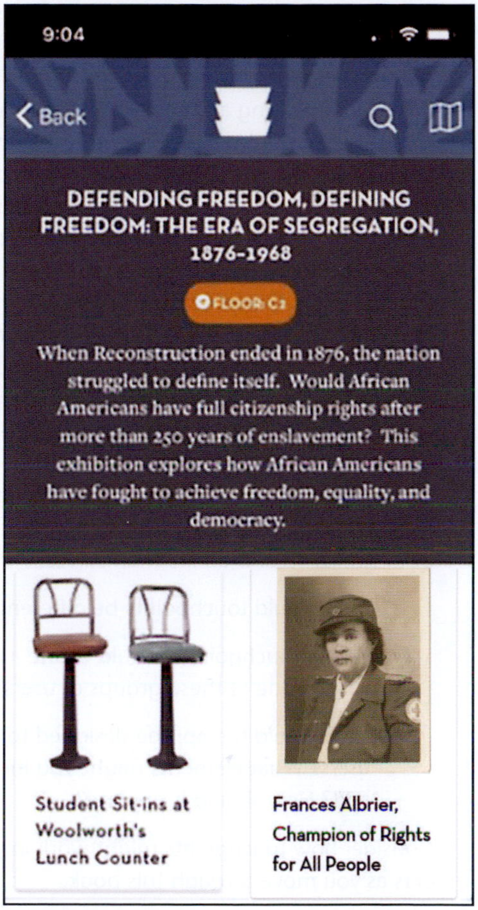

Assessing touchpoints can be a large or small endeavor, depending on the size of the multimodal project. In one major study, a team of designers at a university hospital in Norway evaluated and mapped the dozens of touchpoints (and waiting times) that a breast cancer patient needed to engage with, from their first appointment with a general practitioner to their diagnosis, and then redesigned the four-month process down to a four-day process. Identifying touchpoints is critical for designers so that they can take advantage of multimodal opportunities to best reach their audiences. It allows them to see where they can interact with users and how they might utilize words, images, sound, and other modalities to achieve their rhetorical goals.

Figure 1.8 Touchpoints in the App for the National Museum of African American History and Culture in Washington D.C.

We introduce the concept of touchpoints here because we will use it throughout the book to assess your understanding of making multimodal projects—either through a short analytical exercise (such as the one that follows) or through application to your own project.

◎— **Touchpoint: Understanding Multimodal Processes**

Imagine describing all the points of interaction that an airline passenger must encounter to book a ticket, get to the airport, go through security, find their gate, board the plane, and upon arrival, disembark, find their baggage, and so on. (If you've never flown before, a bus or train service or some other mode of transportation can be substituted.) How would you redesign such an experience to make it easier and more enjoyable for that passenger, from start to finish? Consider how an app might work: from booking a ticket to using the same app at the gate to board, then using the app to map your location in the new airport and get directions to the correct baggage carousel. How would that app work regardless of your user's ability, age, race, ethnicity, religion, orientation, national origin, or other social or cultural identity? Are they a non-native English speaker? Blind? In a wheelchair? Deaf? Transgender? A parent with a toddler? Traveling with pets? These questions help designers think about how multimodal projects can reach audiences both similar to and unlike themselves:

- How would touchpoints be different for each set of these potential users?

- Which touchpoint(s) could create a diversion from the suggested route for any one of these groups of users?

- How would the app be designed to accommodate all of these potential users? What elements might you incorporate that go beyond written text? How should it operate?

Consider how touchpoints might work in your own writing and designing projects as you move through this book.

How Does Multimodality Work?

All kinds of texts are multimodal: newspapers, science reports, advertisements, billboards, scrapbooks, music videos — the list is endless. Consider, for example, all of the modes at play in a simple commercial — there is usually music, the voice of an announcer, video showing the product, text on the screen giving you a price or a Web address, and often much more. Each of these modes plays a role in the advertiser's argument for why you should buy its product. The music is selected to give the product a certain feel (young and hip, perhaps, or safe and reliable). The gender of the announcer and the tone, volume, and other qualities of her, his, or their voice reflect whom the advertiser is trying to reach. The choice of whether to use video or animation, color or black and white, slow motion or other special effects, are all deliberate *modal* considerations based on what the advertiser is trying to sell and to whom. Although each mode plays a role in the overall message, it is the combination of modes — the *multi*modality — that creates the full piece of communication.

In order to think about how a multimodal text does persuasive/ rhetorical work, it helps to break down the text into different components. To those ends, we're going to introduce you to five terms from the work of the New London Group, a collection of education and literacy scholars who first promoted the concept of multimodal literacies. They outlined five modes of communication — linguistic, visual, aural, gestural, and spatial — which they found could be applied to any kind of element in a text (see Fig 1.10).

Every text is made up of individual **elements**. Elements in a text might include specific words or phrases, colors, and individual images that are used — all of which audiences can read individually — to form an overall, cohesive meaning for the text. Although *element* doesn't seem much more specific than *thing*, it is the placement and relation of the elements in a text that offers meaning for the whole.

The photograph in **Figure 1.9** can be split into individual elements: the beach, the trash on the sand, the garbage can, and the sign on the side of the can. Each of these elements can be broken down and categorized to add up to one ironic whole. Although this is a static photo, it is also easy to imagine adding sound to this image.

Figure 1.9 Elements Combined to Create an Ironic Image
sdominick/Getty Images

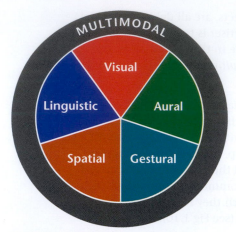

Figure 1.10 The Five Modes of Communication

As an element within this multimodal composition, sound could play an important role in guiding our reading of a text. If this photo were set to the sound of a cheering crowd, it would read differently than if it were accompanied by the sound of chirping birds. The next section will help you better understand how different elements use individual modes of communication to make meaning.

Linguistic Mode

The linguistic mode refers to the use of language, which usually means written or spoken words. When we think about the ways the linguistic mode is used to make or understand meaning, we can consider:

- word choice
- the tone or attitude implied
- the delivery of text as spoken or written
- the organization of writing or speech into phrases, sentences, paragraphs, sections, etc.
- the development and coherence of individual words and ideas

While these aren't the only possibilities for understanding how the linguistic mode works, this list gives you a starting place from which to consider how words and language function. And although we've listed it first—and although it's the mode you probably have the most practice with as a writer/designer—the linguistic mode is not always the most important mode of communication. (Whether it is or not depends on what other modes are at play in a text, what kind of text it is, where and how you are encountering the text, and many other factors.)

The linguistic mode and the ability to use it purposefully matter very much in contemporary communication. Consider the wording on a variety of public signs posted during the coronavirus pandemic and how they affected everyone's willingness to comply. Elements such as the amount of text, the complexity and tone of the wording, the language(s) used, and whether it encouraged or scared readers into taking particular actions are all rhetorical choices that play an important role in achieving the writer/designers' rhetorical and public health goals. The word choices in **Figure 1.11**, for instance, are simple and focus on the importance of community cooperation, while the language used in **Figure 1.12** is more complex and legalistic, taking a slightly threatening approach. While both examples have roughly the same intentions, the differing uses of the linguistic mode vary in effectiveness for different audiences.

Visual Mode

The visual mode refers to the use of images and other characteristics that readers see. Billboards, flyers, TV/movies, websites, TikTok videos, and even grocery store shelves bombard us with visual information in an effort to attract our attention. We can use this mode to communicate representations of how something looks or how someone is feeling, to instruct, to persuade, and to entertain, among other things. The visual mode includes choices about:

- color
- layout
- style
- size
- perspective

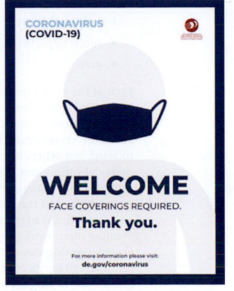

Figure 1.11 **Face Coverings Required Sign**

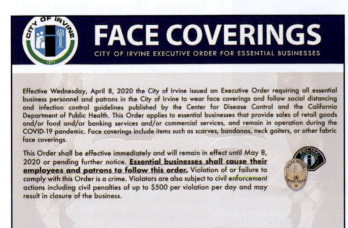

Figure 1.12 **Face Coverings Executive Order**

- framing
- setting/context
- subjects/participants
- gaze

Each of the characteristics we mention here (and many others) can be used by writer/designers to shape how audiences respond to a text and interact with its information. Many of the ways we can talk about the visual mode, such as color and size, seem fairly straightforward, but others like perspective and framing might need a bit more definition here. **Framing** refers to how the most significant elements in a visual are highlighted and how other elements are cut out or pushed to the background. We often do this when we edit and crop photos to emphasize the main subjects we want to share. Framing often works hand-in-hand with **perspective,** which is a way of directing viewers' focus to specific elements. Writer/designers can leverage perspective in intentional ways through strategies like the use of **angles** (such as subjects viewed from above or below), the **gaze** of subjects (where subjects are looking), and the **proximity** (distance or closeness) between the subject and the viewer.

For an example of how these visual strategies work, see **Figure 1.13**, Dorothea Lange's "Migrant Mother." This photo was taken during the Great Depression as part of a photo documentary effort to "introduce Americans to America" and to illustrate the plight of rural poverty. In this image, we see a 32-year-old migrant farm laborer, Florence Owens Thompson, in a concerned, contemplative pose. The tight framing and close proximity to the camera humanizes the participants and helps the audience relate to their plight. Lange's head-on perspective of Thompson, shot from neither above nor below, implies an equality with the viewer. The perspective is further emphasized as viewers follow the line of Thompson's arm to her troubled face, accentuating her condition. Following Thompson's gaze outside the photo frame, we can empathize with the desperation and hopelessness she experienced.

Figure 1.13 "Migrant Mother" by Dorothea Lange, 1936

Library of Congress, Prints & Photographs Division [LC-DIG-ppmsca-50236]

The visual mode is key to the rhetorical success of all kinds of multimodal texts.

For low-vision and blind audiences, the visual mode will often be replaced by other modes. For instance, screen-reading programs that convert written text to speech are an important technology to consider when designing a multimodal text. Versions of texts in Braille, a tactile writing system, may also be made available in print using a Braille typewriter or through a refreshable Braille external device that displays the tiny bumps of Braille for audiences to feel. These aural and spatio-gestural versions of texts are useful tools to help a low-vision reader make meaning of texts, and some of these options can also help other readers who may desire or require transcripts to parse visual texts.

Aural Mode

The aural mode focuses on sound. Whether we are talking about a speech, a video demonstration, sound effects on a website, or the audio elements of a radio or podcast, the aural mode provides multiple ways of communicating and understanding a message, including:

- music
- sound effects
- ambient noise/sounds
- silence
- tone of voice in spoken language
- volume of sound
- emphasis and accent

Although many of us are used to hearing sound all around us every day, we don't often pay attention to how it signals information, including feelings, responses, or needed actions. It's easy to conceive how the words of a spoken message communicate auditorily, but what about the increasingly tense background music in a TV drama or video game, or the sounds that let us know when a computer is starting up, or the tones our phones make when a text message comes in? Whether big or small, each of these aural components conveys meaning for hearing audiences, just as silence or the absence of sound does.

Using the aural mode is increasingly accessible for multimodal writer/designers through projects such as podcasts. Choices about when to incorporate voice-over (including who speaks, what volume, pace, and tone of voice they use), music, ambient sounds, as well as how they might overlap or fade in/fade out all influence the audience's experience. There are infinite possibilities for how these aural choices can be combined to best reach an audience for a particular purpose.

Figure 1.14 An Interpreter Uses Visual and Gestural Modes instead of the Aural Mode

American Sign Language (ASL) interpreter Anthony Diaz relays Gisselle Contreras' retelling of her father's experience as an immigrant in an ICE detention center.

AP Images/Damian Dovarganes

For deaf and hard-of-hearing audiences, the visual mode often replaces the aural or auditory. Whether through American Sign Language (ASL), lip reading, facial expression, or other body (gestural) cues, the visual mode serves as a primary channel for communication. For instance, if you have ever seen an official government press conference, such as those given for public health or natural disaster events, a sign language interpreter is often present to translate officials' messages. As shown in **Figure 1.14**, in addition to the hand movements, interpreters use animated lip, body, and facial movements to convey ideas. Closed captions in videos, such as the one shown in **Figure 1.15**, are one more way of making aural content accessible to deaf and hard-of-hearing audiences and to any audiences who might want or need to read rather than listen.

Spatial Mode

The spatial mode is about physical arrangement. It provides cues about how to navigate and interact with real-world and

Figure 1.15 Closed Captioning

virtual spaces, as well as texts of all kinds. This can include how a brochure opens and the way it leads a reader through the text. For example, in the brochure seen in **Figure 1.16**, the designer created a conference program so that each fold is slightly smaller than the one below it. This allows readers to have a tab for each day of presentations or to see the entire program at a glance by expanding the whole thing. The spatial mode can also refer to the placement of navigation on a website or app to maximize access to content or features for users. This mode helps us to understand

Figure 1.16 Tabbed Conference Brochure Using the Spatial Mode

Edgar Barrantes

why physical spaces such as grocery stores, restaurants, or classrooms are arranged to encourage certain kinds of behavior (such as all chairs in a classroom facing towards the center of the room to encourage discussion and collaboration or towards a podium at the front in lecture-oriented courses). Elements of the spatial mode include:

- arrangement
- organization
- proximity between people or objects
- partitions or boundaries that separate elements

Attention to the spatial mode has become increasingly important as we create content for and interact within online environments such as on smartphones and websites. Writer/designers must pay attention to how content is organized so that audiences can find their way through it without difficulty. Such choices don't just affect ease of use but also impact audience attitudes towards content and its messages. As with all modes, the spatial often works most effectively when it's in coordination with other modes.

Gestural Mode

The gestural mode refers to the way movement, such as body language, can make meaning. When we interact with people in real life or watch them on-screen, we can tell a lot about how they are feeling and what they are trying to communicate. The gestural mode includes:

- facial expressions
- eye movements
- hand gestures
- body language
- spacing/distance and interaction between people

The gestural has always been important in face-to-face conversations and in the theater, but understanding the gestural mode is just as important when communication takes place through virtual interactions on-screen. This has become especially apparent in video conferencing, where participants' every move and expression is visible to others. Whether we are interacting on a Zoom call with colleagues, a gaming raid with friends, or an online chat with family, the gestural mode provides a way of connecting (or showing an inability to connect) to other people.

Gestures can even be interpreted in static images, such as in the 1930s posters in **Figure 1.17** from Franklin Delano Roosevelt's New Deal. Hundreds of posters were created to publicize health and safety, education, and community programs. The poster on the left has a strong horizontal split-frame that divides two statements, one that poses a problem and the other that suggests a solution. In the bottom half, a woman (presumably a teacher?) holds a piece of paper close to John's face while John looks on with discomfort. (Likely, as the poster notes, because he needs glasses.) The body language of the two people helps visually tell the story. The poster on the right has a strong diagonal split from the top of the hammer down to the bright yellow piece of metal on the anvil, a yellow matched by the text. The framing here conveys a sense of directed purpose, immediacy, and action (a split second from now, that hammer will strike home).

Gestures convey a lot of emotion and meaning, as much if not more than words can, although writer/designers should remember that not all people in an audience might be able to move, gesture, or see those gestures in the same way. One cool thing about multimodality is that it can attend to multiple senses, which is sometimes necessary if a reader has a preference or need for one mode of communication over another. When creating multimodal texts, authors should *always* remember that not every reader will be exactly like

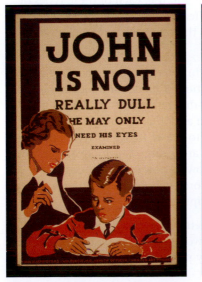

Figure 1.17 New Deal Posters

Library of Congress, Prints & Photographs Division [LC-USZC2-5332], Library of Congress, Prints & Photographs Division, [LC-USZC2-1116]

them, whether in culture, class, race, gender, or ability. A text should be composed so that readers with limited vision, hearing, or touch—among other possible differences within an audience—can still interact with the text. As you analyze and compose multimodal texts, be careful to write/design for as many different users with as many different backgrounds and abilities as possible.

Beyond the important capabilities for making texts more accessible to diverse users, multimodality gives writer/designers all kinds of options for communication and persuasion. As we've shown you in this chapter, each of the modes has its own strengths for sharing ideas with others, but often it is the combination of modes that transforms a text from just informational into something that excites and entices audiences into new ways of thinking and taking action. By leveraging all these available means of persuasion in ways that are right for your own audiences, purposes, and contexts (rhetorical situations), you can compose truly powerful multimodal projects.

Understanding Modes, Media, and Affordances

Let's say you want to share how much you adore your cute dog! You could sketch or paint a picture, but let's face it, you have hundreds of photos that would be much easier to use. Each of these types of pictures in the visual mode are different *media* (singular *medium*) that you can share. The *medium* is the way your text reaches your audience within a specific mode.

Different modes can be expressed in a variety of media. They can be used individually or in a combination of modes and media, because different modes are good at doing different things. We've all heard the expression, "A picture is worth a thousand words." Sometimes it is much easier and more effective to use an image to show someone how to do something or how you are feeling. Say, for example, you want to show your Instagram followers how cute your dog is (see **Fig. 1.18**). A picture will quickly convey more information in this situation than will a written description.

At other times, words may work better than images when we are trying to explain an idea because words can be more descriptive and to the point. It may take too many pictures to convey the same idea quickly (see **Fig. 1.19**).

In other situations where we are trying to communicate how something should be done, it can be more useful to create an animation

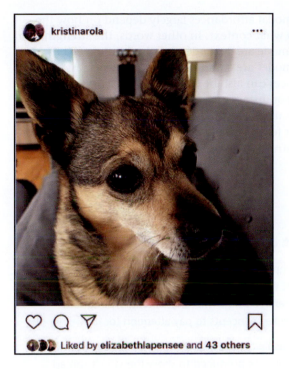

Figure 1.18 Adorable Enid Instagram Post

Kristin Arola

or video (think YouTube videos) that demonstrate the steps in a process, rather than to write out instructions.

These different strengths and weaknesses of media (video, writing, pictures, etc.) and modes are called **affordances** and **constraints**. The visual mode *affords* us the opportunity to communicate movement or emotion in an immediate way, and the linguistic mode *affords* us the time we need to communicate a set of detailed steps. Writer/designers think through the affordances of the modes and media available before choosing the right one for a particular situation.

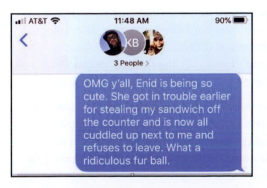

Figure 1.19 Text About Adorable Enid

Kristin Arola

Keep in mind that modal affordances largely depend on how the mode is used and in what context. In other words, the strengths and weaknesses of each mode are dependent on, and influenced by, the ways in which the modes are combined, in what media, and to what ends. Their affordances can also be hindrances to some audiences you want to reach. For instance, the visually brief *emoji* can sum up an entire conversation in a single image, but those readers with less emoji literacy or fewer visual abilities might not understand (or might even misconstrue) what you mean.

CASE STUDY

Mapping the Impact of COVID-19

Although we've given you examples in this chapter of how each mode works on its own to communicate, we want to provide an extended example of how all the modes work together in a single multimodal text. Throughout this case study, we highlight the key concepts to pay attention to.

Figures 1.20–1.22 show data visualizations of COVID-19 infections during Summer 2020. Each visualization was produced to show the virus's spread and the reasoning behind protective measures such as the closure of schools, businesses, and public spaces. The public, government, and health specialists needed rapid access to these visualizations, so they were made freely available online and in a mobile version as well. (This brief description of the text's audience, purpose, and context is called a **rhetorical situation**, which we will discuss more in Chapter 2.) These examples illustrate the affordances of modes for a particular text. The **visual** and **linguistic** modes are primary here. However, both **spatial** and **gestural** modes play prominent roles, and accompanying **aural** resources, in the form of TV, radio, or online streaming press conferences or screen-readable content, are often available.

Although each of the four examples shown in this section contain linguistic content, **Figure 1.20** is the most word/number-heavy. Linguistic descriptions are used for the title and data of the report (COVID-19 Race and Ethnicity Data), the sub-heading (All cases and deaths . . .), the row and column headers, as well as table data and explanatory content at the bottom.

This straightforward table also uses the visual and spatial modes. The use of a blue title and table header calls attention to the text's purpose and provides overview information, while the light gray text at the bottom does not distract from the primacy of the table's data. Notice how the size of the text gets

COVID-19 Race and Ethnicity Data

July 21, 2020

All Cases and Deaths associated with COVID-19 by Race and Ethnicity

Race/Ethnicity	No. Cases	Percent Cases	No. Deaths	Percent Deaths	Percent CA population
Latino	150,960	55.6	3,532	45.2	38.9
White	47,871	17.6	2,384	30.5	36.6
Asian	15,253	5.6	1,021	13.1	15.4
African American	11,717	4.3	672	8.6	6.0
Multi-Race	2,014	0.7	42	0.5	2.2
American Indian or Alaska Native	616	0.2	28	0.4	0.5
Native Hawaiian and other Pacific Islander	1,632	0.6	40	0.5	0.3
Other	41,644	15.3	97	1.2	0.0
Total with data	271,707	100.0	7,816	100.0	100.0

Cases: 425,616 total; 153,909 (36%) missing race/ethnicity

Deaths: 7,949 total; 133 (2%) missing race/ethnicity

*467 cases with missing age

**Census data does not include 'other race' category

Figure 1.20 COVID-19 Race and Ethnicity Data for California, July 21, 2020

smaller as readers move from top to bottom (this is called an informational hierarchy), visually indicating what is most and least important to read.

Spatially, the separation between the title and the table reinforces the graphic's subject. The gridlines within the table help readers move down or across to compare cases or deaths by various races and ethnicities within California. The use of white space within the columns provides visual breathing room so that readers can easily separate information.

While it uses many of the same modalities, the COVID-19 Dashboard from Johns Hopkins University shown in **Figure 1.21** presents a more detailed, multimodal, and interactive text. Through the **gestural** mode, users can zoom in from global-level data to individual states and counties. Clicking (another gestural move) on the "COVID-19 Status Report" opens a detailed, highly visual pop-up window (**Fig. 1.22**) that includes interactive graphs and icons about local hospitalization numbers, cases by demographics, and infection trends over time.

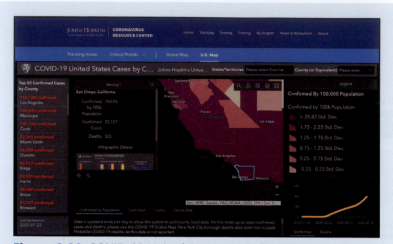

Figure 1.21 COVID-19 United States Cases by County

Johns Hopkins University

With so much content available, the writer/designers kept linguistic content to a minimum so as not to overwhelm readers. As users scroll or zoom the map, only larger towns and cities are marked. Further descriptors and data don't appear on the map itself, but instead are available in small pop-up windows to reduce visual and spatial clutter.

A majority of the information is conveyed visually through size (to indicate level of importance), color (to differentiate severity), framing (the central map

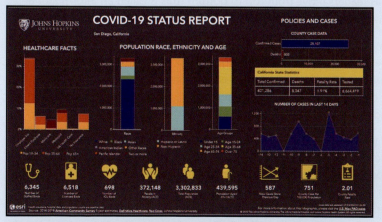

Figure 1.22 COVID-19 Status Report, San Diego, California

Johns Hopkins University

is framed into the webpage). For example, a bright red color, with its connotations of illness, shows statistics in the list of Top 50 Confirmed Cases by County, and a color-coded legend indicates numbers of infection per 100,000 residents so readers can visually compare the status of neighboring states and counties.

In these examples, meaning is made through a combination of modes. Additionally, while sources for COVID-19 information were widely available during early stages of the pandemic, the multimodal affordances (and accurate data) of the Johns Hopkins dashboard made it a credible, engaging, and primary source for millions of users. As you become more aware of how others use a variety of affordances in their texts, you can incorporate these strategies more purposefully and rhetorically into your own writing/designing.

Multimodal Affordances

One way to think about the different modes of communication is as a set of tools. You may not use all of them for a single project, because each mode has its own strengths and weaknesses in specific situations—just as a wrench is more useful in fixing a faucet than a hammer is. Like the tools in a toolbox, though, modes can sometimes be used in ways that weren't intended but that get the job done just as well (like a screwdriver used to pry open a paint can). Every text uses multiple modes of communication and media to make its meaning, and each use of modes and media has affordances that help writer/designers make meaning through them.

The Twitter profile in **Figure 1.23** has a lot of words (the linguistic mode), but the colors, layout, profile pictures, tweet sequence, and prominence of photo-rich tweets (visual and spatial modes) play a big role in how users read and understand each page. Also, the strict 280-character limit for tweets is an affordance of the site, keeping everything quick to skim and easy to read. However, this also *constrains* the way communication happens, offering lots of opportunity for quick broadcasts of ideas but little opportunity for discussion or civilized debate. But hashtags, which allow users to follow a single thread of ideas, are an affordance of many multimodal platforms that can help bring cohesion to the noise of social media.

Figure 1.23 NoDAPL Twitter Feed

◉— Touchpoint: Mode, Media, and Affordance in Everyday Texts

To get a better sense of how prevalent multimodality is in all texts, and how different modes and media draw on their affordances to communicate to readers, collect and/or list texts of any kind that you come across in your daily activities. These might include anything analog or digital, such as a social media post, receipt, text message, flyer, business card, email, meme, website, book, video, song, advertisement, or photo. If you choose to make a list via social media, create a hashtag to keep track of them. If you're working as a class, use the hashtag to create a class record that you can analyze together.

Describe what modes and media the texts use. Count the number of modes that texts use, and see what patterns you can discover across the texts.

- Are they similar types of texts?

- Do they come from a similar time period, location, or publication?

- Are they making similar kinds of arguments?

- Which two texts are the most different from each other?

- How are the modes used in those texts? Which text uses the affordances of its media elements in the most surprising or unusual way? Are there any texts that are using modes and media in ways that seem counterproductive?

- How might you suggest the writer/designers of these texts revise?

write/design! assignment

Mapping Your Multimodal Process

This chapter has been about introducing you to the concepts of multimodality, which might be new for you, but it has also been about informing you that designing multimodal texts is based on a writing process that you are likely already familiar and comfortable with. Writers create with ease certain kinds of texts that they write often. Do you write a lot of emails? Twitter updates? Text messages to your friends or relatives? Do you write reports for work? Make presentations for clients? Write handwritten receipts for artwork you sell? Post updates to the subreddits you follow? You likely do these tasks without thinking about them because they've become routine for you—you know the formula for writing the text, you know the people (or kinds of people) who will read this text, you know exactly how they will use it, and so on. So the process of writing has become automatic, something you don't stop to think about. This assignment is meant to help you

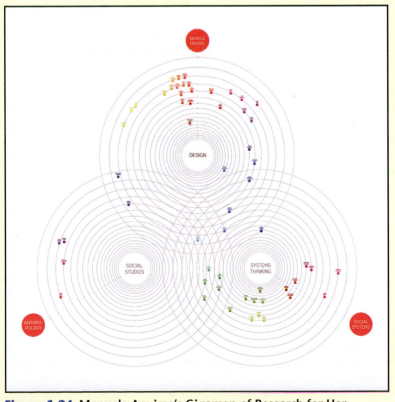

Figure 1.24 Manuela Aguirre's Gigamap of Research for Her Dissertation Project

Manuela Aguirre

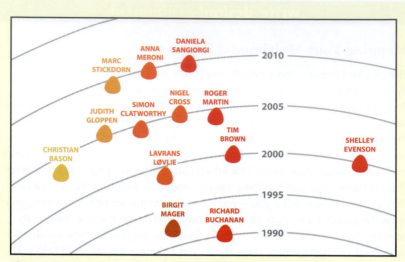

Figure 1.25 A Zoomed-in Portion of Manuela's Gigamap

Manuela Aguirre

realize the scope of things, interactions, and situations in which you write so that you can attend to the different processes, places, services, texts, and events that your writing functions within the next time you sit down to write/design.

Think for a moment of the last major writing or design project you undertook: for a class, for work, for a local organization or club, or just for fun—this project could be as simple as creating a flyer for your sports team, designing invitations for your wedding, writing a paper, or creating a website for your hobby. Now that you have a project in mind, write down as many parts or steps as possible. Next, you'll want to sketch out how those parts connect to one another and to the process as a whole you'd need to complete that project.

Congratulations; you have just started a basic version of what's called a **gigamap**. Gigamaps are *big* maps used by designers to document everything they can about a system, which might include people, places, events, processes, services, tasks, texts, or experiences. In other words, gigamaps help you visualize your process.

Gigamaps start out scrawled on really large pieces of paper—rolls of paper, if you have access to those, or you can use a dry-erase board, a giant piece of cardboard you might have handy, several poster boards taped together—as long as you don't start on a computer. (The process of mapping is more fruitful when you begin in analog form, and using paper is easier if you are collaborating with others, which often happens in design and large writing projects.) Do an image search online for gigamaps to see a variety of examples—they're too large to recreate in detail in this book, so we recommend exploring them in zoomed-in detail on a computer.

What do you include in your writing-process gigamap? Literally everything you can think of that relates to the *who-what-when-where-how* of the project you thought of a moment ago. We have adapted this assignment from Norwegian designer Birger Sevaldson, who created gigamapping, and we offer the following tips adapted from his guidelines to help you start:

- **Nothing is irrelevant:** Deactivate any filter you might have about relevance to the task.
- **Nothing is uninteresting:** Even the smallest detail is interesting in its own right. Search and hunt for it. Look for the smallest details in a chain of events.
- **Strive for information richness:** Work toward a minimum of 100 entities on the map. If you don't have enough, stop filtering yourself or zoom out on your perspective.
- **Don't talk too much—write and draw:** Don't worry about wasting paper. Don't plan the mapping but allow it to develop organically. Don't get trapped in conversations on what the map should look like or what should be included; just include it.
- **Start anywhere:** Start to unfold at any detail. Avoid a central nucleus. Centers of gravity will be found or generated later. Avoid gravitating to hierarchical structures.
- **Activate existing knowledge:** Do not research information in the beginning. This will stop your flow before you even have started. Use your existing knowledge and map it out completely. Then identify what is insufficient and what is speculative and plan your information-gathering research accordingly.
- **Messy is good:** Do not let your inner designer take over the process too early. Let it be as messy as the reality you try to cope with.
- **Mix it up:** Strive to produce a deep map that contains many layers of different information. Allow for different ways of representing information in the map.

Finding and creating relations between different types of information that seem totally unrelated is one of the goals in gigamapping. Therefore, once you have a draft of your gigamap:

- **Create relations:** Use the mapping to create relations that are not there today. What relations should be created to make the system function better? A simple line is not sufficient. Arrows indicate directions of relations. Use additional font variations and color coding. Use other types of relations like proximity or sequencing. Put labels with small descriptive texts or other notes onto the relations and not only onto the entities.
- **Analyze and be critical:** Search for points and areas where there are possibilities for doing things better. Search for possible new relations, intervention points, and innovations in your writing system for this project.

- **Switch media:** Redraw the mapping on your computer and plot it out in large formats to continue working manually. Then repeat the process with new iterations.
- **Share with others:** Present your gigamap to others working on similar projects, in a studio, classroom, study space, work space, or so on, to explain what you've gleaned about your own writing and design process, and what you might improve on as you begin a new multimodal project. What surprised you about how your writing/designing process expanded? How were people, places, or tasks grouped? Why were those groupings important? And so on.

write/design! option: Multimodal Literacy Narratives

We bet you have plenty of experience with multimodality, whether you realize it or not. This assignment asks you to consider who you are as a multimodal reader, writer, and designer. Maybe there was a special book or teacher or performance you saw growing up that struck a chord with you? Or maybe there is a social media app you can't put down, or a game you can't stop playing, or a series that you can't stop binging? Tell a short story about your use of and interaction with multimodality in the world.

Some questions that might help you think about a topic:

- Is there a particular text that stands out in your memory?
- Have you had a good (or bad) experience in learning to do something? Has it been in the classroom? Online? Recreationally?
- What barriers to reading, writing, listening, or using have you encountered as an audience member? Why?
- How do multiple modalities shape your ability to process and interpret information? Which are your most and least favorite, and why?
- What are the ways in which you use multimodal texts to navigate life in and outside of work or school?

Compose a narrative in whatever medium you want that includes any combination of modes—but it has to include at least three different modes at once. The story should tell about your engagement with some kind of multimodal text(s). You can search for examples online using key phrases such as "literacy narrative" or "multimodal literacy narrative" or "technology narrative."

How Does Rhetoric Work in Multimodal Projects?

2

Have you ever been walking through a coffee shop or past a campus bulletin board when one flyer, among the hundreds of flyers you see every day, stands out so much that you can't help but stop and read it? Have you ever been rushing to a meeting when your favorite song starts playing, and you have to listen to it before you can enter the meeting? Have you ever found a video or meme so exciting or funny that you have to immediately share it with your friends? These multimodal texts are captivating—they capture your attention and encourage you to interact with and share them.

Chances are the multimodal texts that caught and held your attention are the ones that used the most intentional design choices. These are the kinds of texts we want you to build. In this chapter you will learn how to analyze multimodal texts to discover how effective design choices are made for different texts in different situations.

Writer/designers have a wide variety of options for creating a persuasive text. What makes a text effective depends on a number of factors: What is the author's reason for creating the text? What audience is the author trying to reach? In what place, time, or situation is the text being created? Analyzing these factors will help you understand the projects of other writer/designers and will help you create your own multimodal texts.

Rhetoric and Multimodality

When we talk about "effective" or "successful" texts, we're talking about rhetoric. Texts need to be created for a purpose, to persuade an audience toward change in some way; **rhetoric** is the study of making texts, like **Figure 2.1**, that effectively convince an audience to think, believe, or take some kind of action. Echoing that old philosophical question—if a tree falls in the forest and no one is around to hear it, does it make a sound?—if a text doesn't induce change, then it isn't rhetorically successful. *Successful* multimodal persuasion is what this book is about.

33

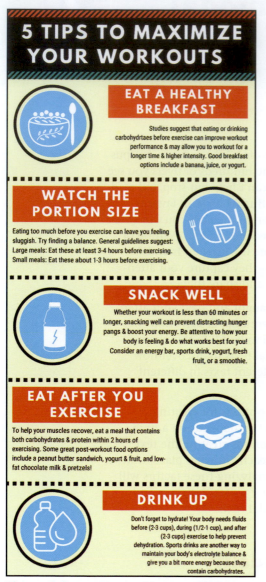

Figure 2.1 An Effective Multimodal Flyer

Courtesy of Angela Wilson

You're probably familiar with some forms of persuading others to take action in favor of an author's viewpoint, such as when an advertisement tries to persuade us to choose a particular political candidate, a new summer outfit, a different brand of toothpaste, a recycling option, or an event to attend. Sometimes this change is more subtle and the action is less explicit, such as when reading a novel gives us a better understanding of the human condition (or simply causes us to relax), or—as in the COVID-19 infection rates example in the Chapter 1 Case Study on page 24—when government or academic institutions offer information to help audiences be more cautious in daily interaction with others.

As readers, we are influenced to act based in large part on how effectively a text persuades us. Let's think about a musical example. While a musician probably has many hopes for a song—that it speaks to people and is artistically meaningful, for example—one hope is that listeners will enjoy the song enough to regularly stream it (which earns money for the artist). Whether or not listeners click on a song depends on a lot of things: whether they like the song's lyrics, whether the song speaks to them in some way, whether it's on the platform they use, and the like. The song's author and producer had to think through all of these possibilities when creating and distributing the song. In the end, they have created a text that asks readers to make a choice. A particular listener's choice may be to do nothing (not to listen to or buy the song), but that's still a choice.

Our reactions typically depend on how well an author is able to address the **rhetorical situation**. The rhetorical situation is the set of circumstances in which an **author** creates a text. Authors have to pay attention to three key factors if they want to be effective communicators: their intended **audience**, their **purpose** for communicating, and the **context** in which their text will be read or used. The genre is also important to consider, and we will address that concept more in Chapter 3.

Analyzing a Rhetorical Situation

Understanding the situation in which an author composed a text can help us better understand a text's meaning and make judgments about its effectiveness. Who was the author? Why did they compose this text? When and where was it composed? Whom did the author want to reach? You may never know everything

Figure 2.2 A Quick Rhetorical Analysis of a Parody

On *Saturday Night Live* (a television show known for its comedic sketches), comedian Maya Rudolph offers an impression of Vice President Kamala Harris and her signature off-the-cuff hand gestures to satirically analyze the vice presidential debates (purpose) for viewers' entertainment (audience) during the 2020 election cycle (context).

Top photo: MediaPunch Inc/Alamy

there is to know about the author's intended purpose or audience, and there isn't always (or ever) a "right" answer when analyzing a text. What we can do is learn how to analyze texts so that we can better understand or hypothesize about how a text works and why.

Thinking through the rhetorical situation like this is called **rhetorical analysis**. Rhetorical analyses can result in texts of their own (such as papers, presentations, or multimodal projects), but they can also function as research for your projects. If you can analyze how a text works, you can often apply that understanding to the design of your own text. A rhetorical analysis is a method of describing the following:

- the *audience* an author wants to reach (the *who*);
- the *purpose* an author has for communicating to that audience (the *what* and *why*);
- the *context* in which an author wants to communicate that purpose or call for action (the *when* and *where*);
- the writing and design *choices* an author makes in a text that draw on audience, purpose, and context (the *how*).

These fundamental concepts (*author, audience, purpose*, and *context*) and questions (*who, what, when, where, why*, and *how*) help us perform a rhetorical analysis. Let's look at each of these areas in greater depth now, followed by a closer look at how to analyze design choices to help determine a rhetorical situation.

Author

The terms *writer, designer, **author***, and *composer* mean the people who make the texts. When exploring authorship of a text, sometimes it will be quite clear—say, in the case of a signed letter to the editor—while at other times you will have to make an informed guess and rely on the implied author. Consider, for example, a visual advertisement for Starbucks. A team of designers (the actual author) composed it, yet the audience assumes Starbucks (the implied author) is the one sending the message. There are other texts, such as a concert flyer, for which you likely will have no idea who the actual author is, but you can probably say a lot about the implied author based on the design of the text.

In the case when you are authoring a text, you know exactly who the author is, of course. But you also have a rhetorical situation in which you have to choose your design elements and genre carefully, so as to best reach the audience you intend. When you're composing, you can ask yourself these questions to make sure you are achieving your purpose and establishing credibility as an author.

- How do you (as an author) establish personal or brand credibility? What multimodal elements make your text trust-worthy? Does it matter for your audience?

- Does the author (you or the brand) have a certain reputation? Does the text work to support this reputation, or does it work to alter this reputation? Which is needed in this particular rhetorical situation?

- What other types of information in the text (historical, biographical, genre-based, research-based) will help you convince readers of your or the brand's credibility, character, and reputation?

As with the Starbucks example, sometimes the fact that you are the author is irrelevant to the composition process if the audience doesn't care or doesn't need to know that you are the actual author—because the audience sees a corporation, group, or some other collaborative entity as the implied author. So, as author in that situation, you need to analyze the mission and vision (the purpose) of the group you are speaking, designing, or writing for and work seamlessly as part of the whole. Your rhetorical analysis skills will come in handy just as much when you are writing/designing as they do when you are reading multimodal texts.

Audience

The audience is the intended readership for a text. There may be more than one intended audience, and there may also be more than one actual audience. Consider a pop-country song playing over the sound system at a store. The songwriter's intended audience is likely pop-country fans, and their secondary audience may be pop or country music fans. Yet, in this context, the actual audience is anyone who happens to hear it.

There are many different types of audiences, such as *stakeholders*, *teachers*, *peers*, *clients*, *readers*, and others, but all these terms refer to the person or people who are the intended readers, users, or recipients of created texts. Often these terms are dependent on the rhetorical situation of a text. *Stakeholders*, for instance, refer to people who have some interest or concern in a project because of

Write/Design Toolkit

See "What Does Your Audience Need?" on page 171 for more on appealing to your audience.

the way it would impact them. *Clients* are typically people from an organization that a writer/designer is working for and who are directing or influencing what is said and how, but they are not always the primary audience for it.

For example, Cheryl has worked on projects funded by the National Endowment for the Humanities (NEH), an agency of the U.S. government that supports humanities-based projects by providing federal grants to researchers. However, Cheryl made writing and design choices in consideration of her *primary audience*, the scholar-teacher communities in which she works because they were the ones who would most actively use the project. The project would also impact the public by making research more available to non-academics. So, NEH is a *stakeholder* and *secondary audience* that expects certain kinds of reporting and deliverables on such projects in exchange for funding, and the public is a *secondary audience* of the project because they would benefit from its outcome.

In a rhetorical analysis, your job is to pay attention to the intended primary and secondary audiences. While it is not necessarily your task to consider how the text will function if read by those outside the intended audience(s), doing so can sometimes be illuminating.

When analyzing audience, consider these questions:

- Who is the intended audience?
- Who might be the secondary audience(s)?
- What values or opinions do the primary and secondary audiences hold?
- How does the author use design elements to appeal to these values or opinions?
- What content or level of detail will these audiences expect?

◎— Touchpoint: Analyzing Audience

What audiences want from a text depends on their needs—in the case of the *SNL* skit example in **Figure 2.2** (p. 35), an audience wants comedic sketches about political figures that help to lighten the mood during an often-divisive campaign season. But what about other audiences' needs in different types of multimodal texts?

In **Figure 2.3**, a student in one of Kristin's classes drew this draft of a roller derby poster with pen and ink for a class assignment. The primary or intended audience

Figure 2.3 Hand-Drawn Flyer for Roller Derby
Nicole Schmidt

Figure 2.4 Final Draft of a Roller Derby Flyer
Huizi Li

would be parents of roller derby players, as signaled by the words, "Parent's Night: Be there or be square, 'rents!" But a secondary audience for this poster could be other students, teachers, business owners, and sports enthusiasts who like roller derby in the small college town. Based on the hand-drawn design and the simple two-color graphics, what kinds of cultural and social values do you think the collective audiences of this poster might have? Would these audiences have anything in common with each other beyond roller derby?

What about **Figure 2.4**? It is also a roller derby flyer, but the writing and design are different from the hand-drawn example. Who are the primary and secondary audiences for this flyer? How might the different design values appeal to these different audiences? Or are the audiences between the two flyers actually that different? Even when a text is not designed with the language we may read or speak, we can often interpret its audience, purpose, and context based on the way multimodal elements are placed spatially. (These familiar usages are called genre conventions and will be discussed more in Chapter 3.)

Purpose

Purpose answers a single question: What is this text meant to accomplish? Describing a text's purpose may sound somewhat simplistic, yet it is important to consider a range of possible intentions—while there may be a large-scale purpose, there often are also secondary purposes. For example, a billboard for a local steakhouse has the primary purpose of attracting new clientele, but it may have the secondary purpose of solidifying existing customers' opinion of the restaurant as a fun-loving family establishment.

Purpose always plays a crucial role in analyzing and creating texts; without a clear purpose, a text is useless as a piece of communication. When analyzing purpose, consider these questions:

- What do you consider to be the overall intention for the text?
- What multimodal elements lead you to this conclusion?
- Might there be one or more secondary intentions? Why do you think so?

The purpose of the breast cancer awareness graphic in **Figure 2.5** is fairly easy to determine: The lemons serve as visual representations for breasts, and each lemon is visually modified to show a symptom of breast cancer. The ad campaign, Know Your Lemons, was designed by Worldwide Breast Cancer, a nonprofit organization that uses multimodal design to educate and empower in ways beyond words, particularly for audiences that have low literacy rates or that face cultural and social taboos in talking about breasts or cancer.

> **Write/Design Toolkit**
>
> Refer to "Choosing How to Work with Technologies" on page 169 for help choosing the technologies that best suit your specific purpose.

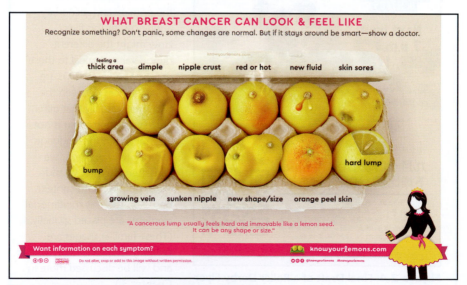

Figure 2.5 Breast Cancer Awareness Graphic
Image provided courtesy of Know Your Lemons Foundation, www.knowyourlemons.com

⊙— Touchpoint: Analyzing Purpose

Think Indian is a public service campaign that, according to the American Indian College Fund (AICF) website, "tells the story of how America's 32 accredited tribal colleges and American Indian students are combining traditional Native solutions with modern knowledge to solve contemporary problems." The ad in **Figure 2.6** was run in major media publications, such as the *New York Times Magazine* and *O*. The primary audience is donors, and the purpose of the ad is to solicit support for the AICF. A secondary audience could be people who identify as American Indians who may not have been aware that the AICF existed, or who want to attend college but weren't sure their ideas mattered. So, the primary stories, imagery, and purpose presented in this campaign can have a secondary influence on this audience.

Consider the design of the ad and how it achieves the AICF's purpose. Perhaps conduct some research on the Think Indian campaign and the AICF and sketch out another possible version of this advertisement that has the same purpose as this one.

This bold white font contrasts sharply with the mute gray background, creating strong emphasis. Why would the idea of "native art made with looms and laptops" be such a strong focus of this ad? What does this say about tradition and technology and about how the purpose is being conveyed?

How does the pop of red against the black-and-white background and figure speak to the purpose of the text?

Notice the city skyline buildings are drawn in with a more traditional native pattern. How does this design, in contrast to the background image, identify a cultural context? What purpose does this design choice achieve?

This small blurb contains donation information. Does it support the primary or secondary purpose of the ad?

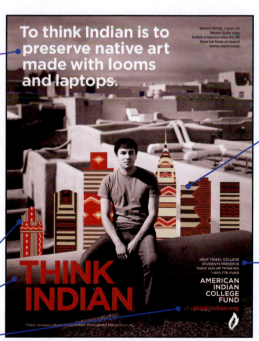

Figure 2.6 Annotated Ad for the Think Indian Campaign

Courtesy of the American Indian College Fund

Context

Context can be quite broad, but it refers to where and how a text will be read or used. It may be physical, such as *where* the text is published or distributed (in an academic journal at a library, for example, or in your Instagram feed), *how* it is meant to be read (while sitting at a desk with one's full attention on the pages, or at a quick glance while scrolling through your phone), *what* surrounds it (similar academic journal articles, other advertisements, an article about dining in Portland), or *when* it was made (in a different decade or during a time of social change). In these ways, context is social and cultural, taking into account the values of a particular publication or culture, or the important events taking place when the writer/designer was creating the text.

When analyzing context, consider these questions:

Write/Design Toolkit

See "Assessing Technological Affordances" on page 174 for guidance on selecting a medium.

- What is the medium (print, image, video, podcast, etc.)? Why do you think the author chose this particular medium over another one?

- Where did you find the text? What was the publication venue (book, newspaper, album, mobile app, website, television, live event, etc.)?

- What were the historical conventions for this type of text? What materials, media, or publishing venues were available at the time?

- What are the social and cultural connotations within the text? What colors, pictures, or phrases are used? What technologies does the text use?

- How will readers interact with this text? Will they read it on their phone or tablet while walking down the street? On a desktop computer in a public library? On a laptop in their backyard?

It often feels like context is the widest of possible lenses to analyze a text with. The Web comic by Kris Straub, "All Houses Matter," (**Fig. 2.7**) provides an example of context in rhetorical situations. The comic provides the analogy of a house burning in order to illustrate how the phrase "all lives matter" can be a harmful response to "Black Lives Matter." (Throughout the book, where relevant, we use gender-neutral pronouns. We discuss why in the next Touchpoint assignment.)

The Black Lives Matter movement began in 2013 after the acquittal of George Zimmerman in the shooting death of Trayvon Martin. The comic shown in Figure 2.7 was composed in 2014 in response to the BLM movement. In the context of 2020, particularly after the police killing of George Floyd, BLM gained more media attention and public approval. Straub's comic saw increased attention in 2020 (six years after its release) and was shared widely across social media—more than it ever was in 2014. The context of racial politics and the visibility of systemic racism likely explains its increased popularity. Being able to analyze the myriad ways that context plays a role in our communications is important to ensuring that those communications are effective.

Touchpoint: Analyzing Context

In spite of showing no distinguishing characteristics, many readers may have looked at the characters in **Figure 2.7** and assumed they were men. The sociocultural contexts in which many of us grow up often incline us to assume that characters with long hair are female and those with short (or no) hair are men. But there are certainly many women with shaved heads and many men with long hair. So, because we don't really know the context of this character, and the comic doesn't explicitly suggest a gender (nor does it need to), we would refer to each character individually with they/them pronouns when discussing/analyzing this comic.

The Web browser extension Jailbreak the Patriarchy, designed by Danielle E. Sucher, genderswaps all pronouns and gendered words on a website. This tiny Web app replaced "him" with "her," "mother" with "father," and so on. In the cultural and social contexts in the United States, this small linguistic change can have a big impact. Just knowing that such an extension exists—or that Suchor was the first female graduate of a computer programming collective in New York City that places many of its alumnae in top start-up or industry jobs—might inspire a young adult to learn to program and to change the world.

Figure 2.7 Kris Straub, "All Houses Matter"
Kris Straub

Do an online search for Jailbreak the Patriarchy and try it out on a Chrome browser, or if you don't have access to that technology, take any text that includes people, such as a superhero comic or book cover, and quickly redesign it (using whatever materials you have handy—a rough sketch is fine) to swap the genders in the design and the writing. Note that gender doesn't have to be binary—male or female—because it can also be fluid. How does this genderswap change the context of the piece? Does it change the message of the communication at all? Does it extend the meaning to new audiences, or does it restrict the message in unexpected ways?

Analyzing Design Choices

One of the ways we can better understand how writer/designers communicate meaning through multimodal texts is to examine their design elements. As we look more closely at the types of choices a designer makes, we focus on six key design concepts: **emphasis**, **contrast**, **color**, **organization**, **alignment**, and **proximity**. These terms aren't the only ones you could use to talk about design choices—you may come up with some terms on your own or with your colleagues—but they give you a start. We ask you to think about how such choices are or are not effective in each particular rhetorical situation. Below we define these terms and provide a few analytical examples. We put them all together, alongside audience, purpose, and context, in a Case Study at the end of this chapter.

Emphasis

In speech or writing, emphasis means stressing a word or a group of words to give it greater importance. This can be done through a change in tone or volume, or through strategies such as pausing for effect or repeating a key term throughout a text. In visual texts, it means the same thing: emphasis gives certain elements greater importance, significance, or stress than other elements in the text, which can guide readers through the text as a whole in specific ways.

When analyzing an image for emphasis, we pay attention to what we notice first and then ask ourselves why. Look back to the Think Indian ad we showed in the Touchpoint activity on page 41. Where is your attention drawn visually? What strategies does the writer/designer use to emphasize this element? Notice what happens in **Figure 2.8**: When the advertisement is changed to black and white,

Figure 2.8 Design Choices in Think Indian Ads

Courtesy of American Indian College Fund

the words *THINK INDIAN* blend into the background and become less significant. Instead, the focus shifts to the white text at the top left, emphasized because of its contrast against the gray background. The emphasis also shifts away from the words and the drawn building images to the student who is centrally aligned within the image. Given the endless possibilities, why do you think this text's designer chose to make *THINK INDIAN* a large, red, all-caps typeface?

Contrast

Contrast is the difference between elements, where the combination of those elements makes one element stand out from another. Contrast can be created spatially, such as when we move between rooms with different purposes. It can also be created aurally, such as when near silence in a horror film or at a sporting event is suddenly replaced with screaming. Color, size, placement, shape, and content can all be used to create visual contrast in a text. No matter the mode, contrast can be determined by comparing elements in a text and experiencing how they differ. Contrast plays a large role in emphasis, in that the most contrasted element often appears to be the most emphasized. See **Figure 2.9**, which contrasts the size of two elements, focusing our attention on the largest one that takes up the most space. Consider, too, **Figure 2.10**. This sound file shows the peaks and valleys of a music track—such rhetorical choices help create energy and movement in music.

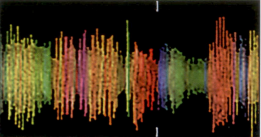

Figure 2.9 Contrast in Gesture   **Figure 2.10** Contrast in Sound

Kent C. Horner/Getty Images   Adam Arola

Color

Color can be extremely helpful when determining emphasis in a visual text. Visual emphasis can be accorded to how bold or large, or how much black compared to the white or gray background is used.

Warm colors such as reds and oranges command more attention than cooler colors like blues and greens.

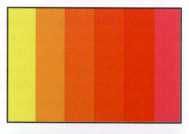

We tend to associate cool colors like blues and greens with water, leaves, cool temperatures, and the sky.

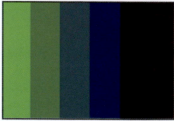

Color doesn't have to mean red, orange, or blue—black and white are colors, too.

Figure 2.11 Color Options

Analyzing a text for color means noticing the colors that are used and to what effect. Do the colors create a certain mood or feeling? Do they emphasize a particular element? Or do they highlight certain elements on the page in relation to each other?

Although color theory indicates that different cultures interpret colors differently around the world, warm colors are usually read as more emotionally intense—think fire, sun, and summer—and are used to elicit emotional reactions in audiences. Cool colors are usually read as calming and are used to create less emphasis than warm colors in a visual composition.

Organization

Organization is the way in which elements are arranged to form a coherent unit or functioning whole. You can talk about an organization of people, which puts people into a hierarchy depending on their job title and department, or about organizing your clothes, which might involve sorting by color and type of garment. You can also talk about organizing an essay, which involves arranging your ideas so as to make the strongest argument possible. Or you can talk about organizing the multimodal elements of a website to support the purpose of the text.

Consider the most recent redesign of your favorite social media site. Where did the designers move the direct-messaging feature? The group chats? The media upload buttons? The editing features? How long did it take you to reorient your gestural navigation to find the information you wanted? Helping users understand the organizational structure of a text is important to ensure audience engagement.

Figure 2.12 features part of an essay in which author Vyshali Manivannan explains her fibromyalgia diagnosis and how she dresses in order to manage pain and represent herself.

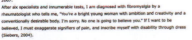

Figure 2.12
Organization in Vyshali Manivannan's webtext, "'But you look so well!': (Un)Professionalizing Chronic Pain Through Academic Dress."

Vyshali Manivannan

The first page of this essay includes a timeline with accompanying images of clothing to represent that moment in time. She organizes her story in a way that makes use of the affordances of the page—that is, readers will read top to bottom and will scroll down as they go, thus they will encounter each description and image sequentially.

Organization is important to consider when you design so that you do not sacrifice usability for aesthetics. In this example, the author manages to satisfy both usability and aesthetic practices by providing a clearly marked organizational structure.

Alignment

Alignment literally means how things line up. A composition that effectively uses alignment controls how our eyes move across a text. Even if we're working with a text that is all words, every piece of it should be deliberately placed. A centered alignment—an easy and popular choice—causes our eyes to move around the space with less determination, as we move from the end of one line and search for the beginning of the next one. A justified alignment stretches the content so that it is evenly distributed across a row; thus the left and right margins remain consistent. This is a popular choice for newspapers because it can make a large amount of text appear neat and orderly. A strong left alignment gives us something to follow visually (because we read left to right in English)—even elements that contrast in size can demonstrate coherence through a single alignment. A strong right alignment creates a hard edge that connects disparate elements. Grouping things in a clear and interesting way can be useful.

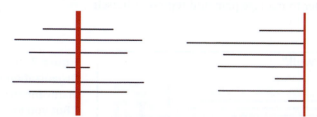

Figure 2.13 Differences in Alignment

Proximity

Proximity means closeness in space. In a visual text, it refers to how close elements (or groups of elements) are placed to each other and the relationships built as a result of that spacing. The relationships created by the spacing between elements help readers understand the text, in part because readers might already be familiar with similar designs of other texts. For example, look at the menu/navigation options of a website you use frequently. Notice how these elements are grouped together (likely at the top of the page, also taking advantage of emphasis and organization) and separated from other parts of the page, helping users know how to access other sections of the site. Proximity can apply to elements in a visual text, including words and images; to elements of an audio text, such as repeating rhythms, verses, and the chorus; and to spatial or gestural texts, such as the placement of actors and the ways they interact or don't interact.

Analyzing proximity in a text means thinking about how elements are grouped together, where they are placed on the page or screen in relation to one another, and how placement suggests purpose. One way to figure out how elements are grouped together into like categories or relationships is to squint your eyes and count how many major groups you see.

How many groupings do you see on the book cover in **Figure 2.14**? Book covers are designed to sell books to readers; they have to present information and content in an interesting, visual, and coherent way. The biggest wording—in large, bold letters on two lines—is at the top of the cover. This is the book title and the most important information. Placed underneath the book's title are the names of the book's editors. You can tell that the titles and names are related because they appear close to each other. The tan line in which the editors' names are presented also clusters these names together. At the same time, the information that appears below the tan line—the

Figure 2.14 The Cover of an Interactive e-Book

Courtesy of Ryan Trauman

publisher and table of contents (TOC)—uses the same color scheme as the editors' names, which is an additional technique used to create relationships. The title and editors are grouped by physical proximity on the page, and the editors, publisher, and table of contents are grouped by proximity of color.

Proximity is also relevant when managing multimedia elements in an animated text such as an audio or video file. Consider how a soundtrack element and a filmic element might need to be presented simultaneously to achieve a text's purpose. Or, think about how annoying it is to the viewer when the audio and video

---

◎— Touchpoint: **Analyzing a Website's Rhetorical Design Choices**

Try the exercise here to analyze a website (and if you want to see how we analyze a specific home page, read the Case Study on page 51, then come back to this Touchpoint activity). Visit your favorite website or app—one whose purpose you are familiar with—and notice the information on the home page. Why do you think it was chosen? What does it say about the primary intended audience and its needs? Take note of the design choices that stand out to you, paying attention to the following:

- What elements does the design of the website emphasize? The logo? A certain picture? The navigation bar? Why would the design of these elements speak to the intended audience?

- How is contrast used on the page? Does the use of contrast help to emphasize certain elements? Does it create a certain feeling or help the designer reach a certain audience?

- How do certain colors emphasize certain elements or encourage certain actions or emotional and cultural responses?

- Notice the organization of elements on the page. What comes first? What comes last? Why do you think the designer chose this order? How does it assist in communicating the context and purpose of the site?

- What elements are aligned on the page? Does this alignment help you navigate the page? How does this choice help the designer communicate the site's purpose?

- How are elements positioned in proximity to one another? Why did the designer place certain elements in close relation and others farther apart? What does this proximity communicate about the website's primary purpose?

don't sync properly. The proximity of the multimedia elements matters a lot to the audience's understanding of purpose.

Writing and Designing Rhetorically

We began this chapter by discussing the rhetorical situation and then moved on to the design choices. However, we can also work the other way around—starting with an analysis of the design choices so as to understand the rhetorical situation. Don't be surprised if analyzing a text's design causes you to go back and say more about the audience, purpose, and context of the text—form and content work together in multimedia texts. Keep in mind that using rhetorical analysis to understand a text may result in a favorable opinion of the text but may also illuminate various problems—the rhetorical analysis may help explain why the text has that "wow" factor, or why it doesn't.

CASE STUDY

Analyzing the Chemeketa CC Website

Our goal in this rhetorical analysis of the Chemeketa Community College website is to figure out what types of design choices were used to effectively respond to a particular rhetorical situation and convey the text's purpose to the audience in a specific context.

Figure 2.15 (p. 52) shows the home page of the Chemeketa CC website. This text, like most college home pages, has two main **purposes**: (1) to brand the college in a positive light, particularly in terms of its educational benefits, and (2) to serve as the portal to a large amount of additional information about the college. College home pages tend to include attractive images and links to information about the college's mission, its cost, its path to career options, its admissions and financial aid policies, its programs and majors, students and faculty, and its location.

The **audience** for the home page is the intended readership: people interested in Chemeketa CC, including current or potential students, sometimes their parents, and faculty and staff. A good designer would try to think of all the different reasons to visit the Chemeketa CC home page and then design the page for these various users.

Figure 2.15 The Front Page of the Chemeketa Community College Website (2020), Featured on a Laptop

Chemeketa Community College

The Chemeketa CC home page is organized into two rows of information. The first row includes the Chemeketa CC logo, a menu, and a search function. The second row includes photos highlighting three students, links to more information about each student, and a "meet the students" link. This simple **organization** is referred to as *flat design* because it minimizes the number of elements that appear on a starting screen. In this particular design, the elements are grouped in close **proximity** to indicate the different sub-purposes each grouping has, and to make it seem like there are fewer blocks of information to choose from. Designers have begun using flat design to prevent audiences from feeling confused or overwhelmed on their sites. From an aesthetic standpoint, users and designers seem to like this trend, but organizationally, it can make finding information difficult.

Analyzing a text within its *historical* and *technological* **context** is important—as our goals, technologies, and media affordances change over time, so does the effectiveness of a particular design. Compare the Chemeketa CC 2000 site (**Fig. 2.16**) with redesigned sites from 2005 (**Fig. 2.17**) and 2012 (**Fig. 2.18**). The assumed size of the screens that **audiences** would use to view websites has changed radically in the last twenty years, as we have moved from midsized, low-resolution monitors to large, high-resolution desktop and laptop screens, and now the use of handheld devices with high resolutions and tiny screens has radically increased. The 2020 version of the Chemeketa CC website in **Figure 2.15** was specifically created to be viewable on computers and mobile devices (see **Fig. 2.19**).

Figure 2.16 2000 Version of the Chemeketa CC Website

Chemeketa Community College

Figure 2.17 2005 Version of the Chemeketa CC Website

Chemeketa Community College

Figure 2.18 2012 Version of the Chemeketa CC Website

Chemeketa Community College

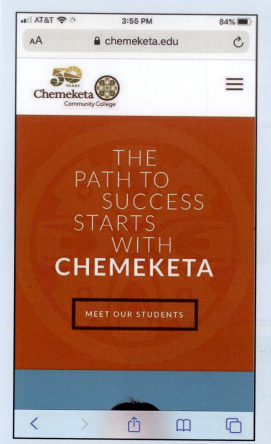

Figure 2.19 2019 Chemeketa CC Website, Featured on a Mobile Phone

Chemeketa Community College

This is called *responsive design* because it *responds* to the device it's being read on. Understanding the technological and historical contexts of multimodal texts helps us analyze how and why a text is designed for particular audiences and contexts.

The **purpose** of community college websites like that of Chemeketa CC has also changed over time—the earlier sites were intended to be portals to attending and working at Chemeketa CC, while the most recent site design shifts importance to telling student success stories. When the site was redesigned to be responsive, Web design conventions had shifted to focus on visuals as the primary mode of communication.

The three student photos shown in **Figure 2.15** are given primary visual **emphasis** on the Chemeketa CC home page from 2020. Simply put, they take over the entire screen. These visual changes can also be noted in the use of **color** throughout the website's history. In early examples, there is no consistent use of color from version to version. The circle logo appears in the 2012 version (**Fig. 2.18**), and the earth tone colors used on the site mimic the logo colors. The 2020 version still uses the logo, but the primary colors of the site itself are much brighter with the earthy tones seen in the text, which **contrast** nicely with the bright colors.

The primary linguistic element—the words "the path to success starts with Chemeketa"—is center **aligned** within its column on both screen sizes (**Figs. 2.15** and **2.19**), drawing our attention to the importance of these words.

Thus, the page is not too busy, like earlier text-heavy versions were (**Fig. 2.17** in particular), and the **audience** can easily see the site's **purpose**, to encourage students to apply for, and attend, Chemeketa Community College. In **contrast**, important information about the college, such as a directory of emails, is hidden in the menu button in the upper-left corner of a mobile user's phone.

With the website's focus on one large block of visuals (the three photos plus the orange text box) and less on written text, **alignment** is a less prominent design choice than it was in the 2000 (see **Fig. 2.16**) version, where many alignments were used artistically to create a collage-type feel. But if we scroll down (see **Fig. 2.20**), we find more linguistic modes represented, which have strong left alignments that create a cleanly organized multi-columned effect.

In **Figure 2.20**, the **organization**, **alignment**, and **color** of visual and linguistic elements designed into two rows, each visually divided into two columns, as well as the **proximity** of the linguistic elements on the left and on the right, suggest how the information is grouped. The left-hand side of the yellow and beige rectangles are meant to grab the **audience's** attention with large headlines—"Students can use our Remote Learning Hub" and "Find a career that fits you." Each of these headlines use **color** to create **contrast** and **emphasis** that draw the attention of the audience. The links on the right-hand side of each rectangle are set off visually through proximity,

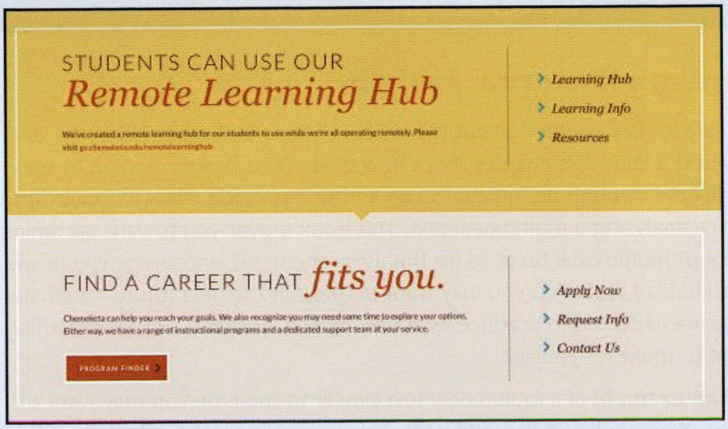

Figure 2.20 Featured Information on the 2020 Chemeketa CC Website

Chemeketa Community College

and the use of the vertical line. The turquoise arrows also work to **contrast** against the background and make the links pop. Considering the **purpose** of the website is to support current students and attract new students, it was smart to emphasize this content. In the yellow section, current students can easily find the Remote Learning Hub and learn more about it, and on the bottom beige section, potential students can find useful information about Chemeketa CC.

Of course, the design of this site, while engaging, doesn't address the needs of every **audience** and **purpose**, which is often difficult in large-scale projects. As we explored this website ourselves, we couldn't, for example, find an email directory listing all faculty and staff email addresses, which is one of the main reasons some **audiences** use a university website. Key information for university website audiences is often buried either accidentally or purpose-fully. Such placement of information (related to the **organization** or page layout) indicates that "buried" items are less important or that designers want to funnel users through particular points of contact. This can be a serious drawback of flat designs that tend to hide information in subsequent pages and can frustrate **audiences**. Performing an analysis of a text's rhetorical situation and design choices can help writer/designers decide which choices they will make in their own texts.

write/design! assignment

Designing a Rhetorical Analysis

We talked a lot in Chapter 1 about the variety of texts that are multimodal, and we've talked a lot in this chapter about how those texts make meaning to specific audiences through design choices an author has made. Now it's your turn to practice analyzing a multimodal text. This book moves you toward becoming an author of multimodal texts, so for this assignment, we encourage you to work with the kinds of texts that you may want to make in the near future—perhaps ones you are expected to produce for a class, event, or client, or just something you want to make for yourself.

1. **Find an example** of a multimodal text similar to the type you may want to design. Your choice of text/artifact for this project is nearly unlimited, unless you have been assigned a specific kind of text from your clients or teacher. If you get to choose any kind of text to analyze, the best projects usually come

about through selecting a topic that is of personal interest to you *and* that is rich in the sort of rhetorical moves and design choices it uses.

2. **Analyze it** using the key concepts you learned in this chapter, with the following questions to guide you (but feel free to expand on these suggestions). Alternatively, you can revisit a text you have created in the past and perform a rhetorical analysis on the project to discover, in retrospect, whether it was as rhetorically successful as you had intended.

   Audience: Who is the intended audience? Who might be the secondary audience(s)? What values or opinions do the primary and secondary audiences hold? Does the author appeal to these values or opinions in any way?

   Purpose: What do you consider to be the overall intention for the text? What leads you to this conclusion? Are there secondary intentions? Why do you think so?

   Context: What is the medium (print, app, Web, video, etc.)? Why do you think the author chose this particular medium over another one? What was the publication venue (book, newspaper, album, television, etc.)? What were the historical, social, and cultural contexts and values of the audience and publication? What technologies does the text use?

   Design choices: What elements do you see or experience first? Last? Why do you think the designer chose this order? What elements are emphasized through organization, color, emphasis, or other strategies? How is contrast used? What elements are aligned? How and why are elements positioned in relation to one another?

3. **Make notes** on your answers to these questions. As you go through these questions, you will want to have your sample text in front of you. Feel free to make your notes multimodally: record yourself talking, draw pictures, type textual notes on top of an image on your computer or tablet screen, even create a gigamap like you did in the Chapter 1 Write/Design! assignment and use large sheets of paper to document your analysis.

4. **Reflect on the text's situation:** After you have completed your initial analysis of your sample texts, read through your notes and decide which parts of your analysis are best supported by the rhetorical and designerly evidence you've collected. Ask yourself what the purpose of your text is and how all the rhetorical and design choices help achieve that purpose. What key examples or elements in the text help you explain its rhetorical situation? How would you organize these elements to explain the text's rhetoric to someone else?

5. **Consider the presentation format:** Now, think about your *own* rhetorical situation as a designer of a multimodal analysis. How might you present your analysis to someone else? Would they prefer it all written down in an essay? Or as a spreadsheet with the key concepts as column headers? Or as a poster?

How can you pull out the main evidence from your analysis to create a cohesive text that presents your reading to an audience? Rather than relying solely on words, this approach allows you to use the affordances of each mode to deliver your argument most effectively.

For example, if you are interested in how acquaintances construct their identity through images on Instagram or profile pictures on Twitter, creating an annotated slideshow of posts might work most efficiently for presenting details of your text.

6. **Compose your multimodal argument** on the effectiveness of these choices using whatever tools or modes are most effective for your own rhetorical situation and then present your multimodal analysis to that audience.

write/design! option: Writing a Rhetorical Analysis

This option asks you to complete a detailed and persuasive analysis of a text and present it as a written essay using "quotations" from the original text. Quotations might include written text as you'd use in a traditional essay, or they could be multimodal elements such as images or embedded video clips. Nearly any multimodal text will work as the basis of your analysis, but here are a few ideas: a single photo or series of photos (such as the photo essays available in online news sites like CNN, *Time*, or the *New York Times*), an advertising campaign, a website, a movie or TV episode, a series of Instagram filters, a YouTube video or channel, a collection of tattoos, a radio program or podcast's use of sound effects, the signage and branding on your campus or for a political campaign, or something else entirely.

Follow the same questions as those posed in Step 2 of the previous write/design option (p. 57) so that you analyze the rhetorical situation of your text based on its written and designed content. When writing up your analysis, plan to use several specific examples from the text in your critique. Consider including images, screenshots, quotes, or other ways of showing your readers pieces of the original text to support your argument. If you are analyzing sound, a gesture, or something that cannot easily be represented in a written essay, take care to describe it in specific detail so your reader can understand your analysis. Remember that you are trying to reveal something about the rhetorical and design choices within the text that perhaps your audience didn't notice or hadn't thought about. Help your reader see what you see in that text and how it matters in making meaning.

Why Is Genre Important in Multimodal Projects?

3

One of the biggest lessons we've learned as authors and teachers is the value of practicing writing/designing for a range of rhetorical situations. Writing/designing is a practice—one that includes analyzing, composing, and revising in different media, modalities, and genres.

You will communicate more persuasively if you come to a writing/designing situation attuned to the specific rhetorical situation, with its particular social and cultural expectations, and then mindfully choose rhetorical strategies. Part of this choosing, and at the heart of excellent writing/designing, lies in an author's explicit use (or breaking) of genre conventions within a rhetorical situation. In this chapter, we focus on understanding the messy concept of **genres** and how authors choose their genres and work within **genre conventions**. We will perform a **genre analysis** on a sample set of texts (which builds on rhetorical analysis from Chapter 2), and you can use that information to decide which kind of text *you* want to compose as an author within your own rhetorical situation.

> **Write/Design Toolkit**
>
> See "Getting Feedback on Your Rough Drafts" on page 194 for help with revising based on feedback.

Genre and Multimodality

One of the best ways to begin thinking about a multimodal project is to see *what* has already been said about your topic as well as *how* other authors have designed their texts on that topic. For instance, you may want to create a text about how students use technology to enhance their learning experience. Before getting started, you'll need to know what's already been said about that topic—an exploratory process that's similar to what you'd do when writing a research paper. Researching your topic is the *what* part of the equation (in other words, figuring out *what* you want to say).

While you're researching your topic, you'll also need to explore *how* other authors are presenting that topic. What combinations of communicative modes do you see in other authors' texts about your topic? What design choices are they making? What genres are they using?

Write/Design Toolkit

For advice on working with technologies, refer to "Choosing How to Work with Technologies" on page 169.

Unless your teacher or client has assigned you a specific genre to work within, you'll want to research multiple genres in multiple media outlets—both academic (texts you'd find in a library database listed under "peer reviewed") and popular (texts you'd find on websites such as YouTube or in bookstores, magazines like *Teen Vogue* or *Wired*, personal blogs, brochures in doctors' office waiting rooms, ads on the sides of buses, etc.). You'll see a different combination of modes and different design choices in each of these texts, depending on the rhetorical goals of the publisher and the author's rhetorical situation.

When examining the *how* of your topic, you'll need to ask yourself:

- How do other authors present your topic?
- Which of their texts seems to address its rhetorical situation most effectively?

Genre

Authors are often responsible for suggesting or choosing the **genre**, a category of communication characterized by similarity in form, style, content, and intent. The concept of genre includes both the formal characteristics of a text (in the case of a recipe, like the one in **Figure 3.1**, an ingredient list and step-by-step instructions) as well as the text's purpose (to provide guidance on how to prepare food). Sometimes genre relates to a text's medium, such as newspapers, albums, or movies, and sometimes we use it to refer to more specific items within a genre, such as horror, romantic comedy, documentary, and so on. Generally speaking, audiences expect something from newspapers that they do not expect from movies, and they expect something from horror movies that they do not expect from romantic comedies. Understanding genre helps us recognize how to group similar texts and understand their communicative purpose.

Understanding Genre Conventions

Genres aren't just static categories; they can morph according to the rhetorical situation, which may include local culture, social agreements and expectations, historical time period, author of the text, audience for the text, and many other influences. Genres are dynamic, but most genres have formal features that tend to remain the same in each use. These features are the **genre conventions**—the features that audiences expect from a text. Conventions of a horror movie, for example, include dark lighting and ominous music.

Figure 3.1 Recipes

The recipe genre features step-by-step instructions, and while we expect certain things from this genre, it can be found in different forms on food blogs, websites, print cookbooks, or newspapers. Recipes can also be passed down verbally through communities.

Angela Buchanan

Readers expect a map, as one type of genre, to be a spatial and visual arrangement of a place with labels for major points of interest. The whole point of maps is for readers to be able to orient themselves geographically (in most cases) to a destination. Maps conventionally include notations for scale, distance, and direction, and also include a legend that defines icons used in the map. Other genre conventions for maps are a title (which indicates its purpose), the name of the cartographer, the date of production, and the projection used in the map. Check out the four maps included in **Figure 3.2**, all produced by the U.S. Central Intelligence Agency at different times and for different purposes, but all focused on the continent of Antarctica. Each of them includes the essential genre conventions for maps mentioned in this paragraph.

As the varying designs of the maps in **Figure 3.2** indicate, genres often contain **subgenres**, or groups of similar genres that all fall under the same category. We know that all of the figures shown are

Antarctica (Small Map), 2016

Antarctic Region (Political), 2001

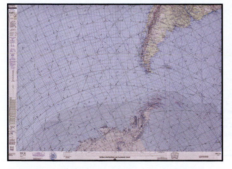

Antarctica Global Navigation and Planning
Chart (Sheet G-24), 1970

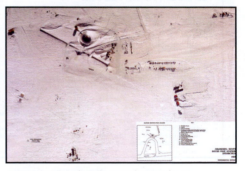

Antarctica South Pole Aerial View, from
Amundsen-Scott South Pole Station, 1983

Figure 3.2 CIA Maps of Antarctica

The University of Texas Libraries, The University of Texas at Austin

maps, even though the genre conventions are designed in different ways for each map. Some map subgenres include (but aren't limited to) artistic, relief, geologic, Z-dimension, street, general reference atlas, and cartograms. Each subgenre of map is designed to fulfill a different rhetorical situation, but all include the essential genre conventions of maps, unless a cartographer's goal is specifically to break the conventions for some artistic or rhetorical purpose.

For instance, one reason a cartographer might want to break convention is to show something that would otherwise be missing or distorted in a map design. Maps typically indicate their *projection*, which refers to their representation of area, distance, direction, and shape. Projection is created based on longitude and latitude and deciding how to represent a spherical planet on a flat, rectangular piece of paper. One of the best known is the Mercator projection, which unnaturally distorts the size of certain areas, making them appear much larger or smaller than they actually are (see **Fig. 3.3**). Many cartographers and critics have suggested different projections that accommodate a more accurate representation of area on maps, such as the Gall-Peters projection, which shows the African continent much larger than in the Mercator map (see **Fig. 3.4**). Some argue that this rendering corrects a false, Eurocentric power dynamic. Or sometimes, because of the situation, your focal point on the map isn't the equatorial perspective—with the Northern Hemisphere at the top and the Southern Hemisphere at the bottom of the flat map, respectively—which we typically see in many world maps. Instead, your focal point is a polar perspective that puts Antarctica at the center of that map (see **Fig. 3.5**). Maps, like any text, change according to our rhetorical situation, and the genres (and subgenres) we choose as authors help us reach our intended audiences more effectively.

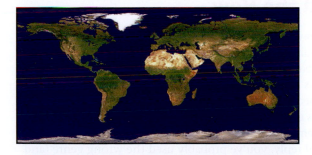

Figure 3.3 A Mercator Map

Among other distortions, this map distorts Antarctica to be larger than the rest of the continents put together.

VanHart/Shutterstock

Figure 3.4 A Gall-Peters Projection Map

This map projection looks purposefully distorted but actually has no distortion at 45° latitude north and south.

NASA

Figure 3.5 An Orthographic Projection Map

Matt Cooper/Shutterstock

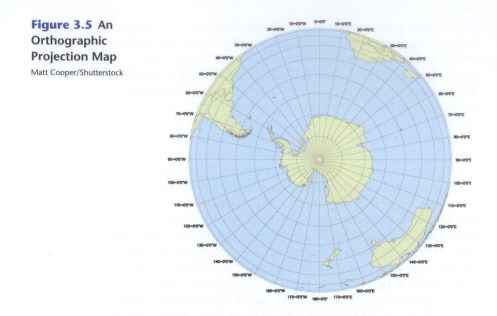

Multimodal Genres: Defining the *What* and the *How*

When authors have a choice of what genre to produce for a project, sometimes the variety can seem overwhelming. At other times, the genre is mandated or seems self-evident. In a poetry writing class, writing a poem is the expectation; in a biology class, writing a lab report is the expectation. In a business setting, if you respond to your supervisor's emailed question about the time of the meeting by printing a memo and putting it in their mailbox instead of sending a quick email reply, you've probably used the wrong genre (and medium) and would send a totally wrong signal—one of passive aggression that may negatively impact your chances at that next promotion. Choosing the correct genre shows that you understand the rhetorical situation and how to persuade and communicate with your audience. In this section, we provide some examples of genre types that multimodal authors might find useful.

Write/Design Toolkit

See "Drafting Your Project: Static, Dynamic, and Timeline-Based Texts" on page 178 for more information.

Static and Dynamic Genres

Static genres are genres we typically associate with analog presentations that are often found distributed in printed forms, such as posters, flyers, brochures, reports, paintings, and the like, but may equally appear in three-dimensional forms, such as statues, architectural models, rapid prototypes from 3-D printers, clothing, and other artifacts. We call these static genres because once they are produced for audiences, they are meant to be read as a singular object, in one glance. That is, they don't move or change radically over time or with user interaction. **Dynamic genres**, on the other hand, do change and are often timeline based or require user interaction to work. Dynamic genres include videos, audio projects, websites, pop-up books, presentations, performances, and the like. In many cases, they are digital, like websites, but that's certainly not a requirement—pop-up books, for instance, have been a popular form of literature for both adults and children for nearly a millennium!

Like all genres, some change categories over time because they change genre conventions. For instance, a gif (graphics interchange format) is a digital genre created for use in the early days of the World Wide Web. Gifs used to be the predominant form of static image on the web because of their small file size, which allowed for easy transmission over data lines. Within a few years after the gif's creation, an animated option was created, which was generally used in ways unrelated to its original purpose. For instance, in the mid-to-late 1990s, the web was filled with animated gifs of mailboxes opening and closing with a letter flying in to signal how to email the site author, or with "Under Construction" signs lighting up to show websites in progress. For expert users of the Web, these animated gifs were annoying at best.

Now, animated gifs are considered the *only* form of gif by most users, and these gifs include photographs strung together or a snippet of film on a loop with snappy captions to help send a message. So, the use of a genre all depends on the rhetorical situation: Are you designing a website for fourth-graders? Or for university teachers? Is it 1999 or 2022? Is your site meant to be ironic or informational? As an author, knowing the context and purpose, along with your audience's tolerance for gifs (or any other genre), will go a long way in persuading them that you know what you're talking (or writing/designing) about.

Genre Structure and Design

In addition to authors choosing whether a static or dynamic genre is most suitable for their rhetorical situation, they can deepen meaning through their structural choices. Written text tends to persuade readers through a **linear** organization—we read one word after the other, forming meaning from words that build into sentences that build into paragraphs. We often make meaning from movies in the same way, watching one scene after another in a linear timeline.

Of course, both written text and movies can also be presented in **nonlinear** structures by their authors.

This is what happens when we have flash-forwards and flashbacks in fiction and nonfiction stories, scripts, films, and other narrative genres. Nonlinearity adds a dynamic dimension to an otherwise linear or timeline-based text, and it thrives in multimodal texts as a meaning-making method. But it requires an audience that either expects, or is willing to explore, this organizational pattern. The audience must then interact with the dynamic text to make sense of it as they piece together the chronology or identify the relationships between the parts and the whole. The title page of a scholarly multimedia piece, "Decolonial Directions" (**Fig. 3.6**), presents an image for navigation that, as the authors describe, represent "the seven sacred directions acknowledged by both Cherokee and Muscogee Creek cultures." The authors explain that "Hovering over and selecting a direction leads to its associated media and placard. We do not provide a specific navigational starting point as a way to highlight the affective experience of non-linearity inherent to the process of decolonization." Readers/viewers can make sense of what may be an unexpected pattern of organization by drawing on previous knowledge of design elements like color and emphasis. In the case of **Figure 3.6**, we've put our mouse over Wudeligv'i and it turns yellow, emphasizing this area and suggesting to us we might click on it to be brought to a new area of the text.

Another method of designing a text that highlights its multimodality as a significant meaning-making technique is **representation.**

Figure 3.6 A Non-linear Title Page

Courtesy of Rachel Jackson and Phil Bratta. "Rivers, Relationships, and Realities of Community Engagement on Indigenous Lands" by Rachel Jackson and Phil Bratta; https://decolonialdirections.org/

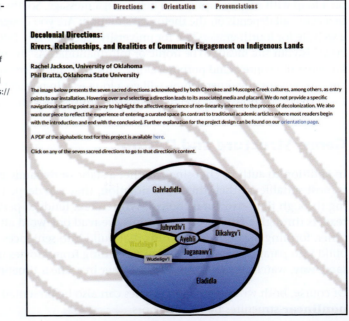

Representation is *re*-presentation, or *re*-designing and *re*-communicating the purpose of a text through multimodal elements. For instance, if you're creating a text about eating habits in different cultures, maybe your text could look like a menu (see **Fig. 3.7**) or a plate with different kinds of food on it.

Your goal is to find a way of representing your topic that adds meaning to your text. This is called a *guiding metaphor*. Guiding metaphors add meaning to arguments by engaging multiple modes. For example, in the Case Study presented at the end of this chapter, Maria Andersen creates a guiding metaphor for her prezi: She uses an illustration of a game board to represent her argument that games promote learning. However, representations don't have to be visual. For instance, if you're working on an audio text, ask yourself whether it's useful for your sound effects to exactly mirror the narrative content—should the cat meow like a typical cat in your piece? Or does the cat represent something else—a lion, a ghost, a guardian angel—that might suggest a different sound effect?

Figure 3.7 A Tourist's Guide to Traditional Filipino Breakfast

A student in Jenny's class wrote/designed an infographic that explains different Filipino breakfast foods. Part of the infographic is designed like a menu and describes how to pronounce the item name as well as offers a description of the dish itself.

Eirein Gaile de Jesus Harn

As an author, if you're having trouble coming up with something that *represents* your idea, try brainstorming things that are *associated* with your idea instead. This strategy can be helpful if the representations you're coming up with seem too literal, too specific, or cliché (for example, if you're writing about love and the only representation you can come up with is a heart). **Association** uses an idea or concept related to your main purposes and uses a part of it to stand for a whole (also called *synecdoche*); in multimodal texts, a multimodal element can act as a simile for the whole text's purpose. Authors use association all the time in everyday texts. How often have you seen Mickey Mouse's ears used to mean the Disney Company, for example, or heard the term *9/11* used to refer to the September 11, 2001, terrorist attacks in the United States?

Figure 3.8 Student-Designed Movie Poster Link

Elyse made this movie poster after brainstorming the best ways to visually link to her film projects on a portfolio website. Clicking on the image brings the user to the movie itself.

Elyse Canfield

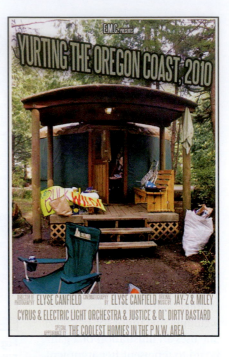

Elyse, a student of Kristin's, was writing/designing an online portfolio that showcased her photography and videography skills. While she had little trouble composing the photo pages, she wanted to find a unique way to link to her short films. With Kristin, she brainstormed the various genres, such as trailers, through which filmmakers showcase their films. She realized that movie posters would work better, since in a single glance a reader associates a movie poster as a stand-in to advertise a full-length movie. Elyse searched online for movie posters and began to compose posters for her films following the genre conventions (see **Fig. 3.8** for one example). Each poster linked to the film in her portfolio.

◉— Touchpoint: Finding Your Genre

Like Elyse's example shows, it's important to find the right genre for your project. Sometimes the genre is defined for you—a stakeholder asks for a report, a documentary, a brochure, a flyer, a song, a memo. If that's the case, your job is a little easier than if you are presented with a scenario where you have to figure out which genre to use.

But let's say a client wants you to help them market their book, and that's all the instruction you are given. In a case like this, you need to analyze the rhetorical situation of this book, as well as similar books, to figure out what genres will best help the readership of the book learn about it. You might compose flyers, create a Twitter and Instagram handle, a YouTube or TikTok account, or a press packet, or set up interviews and send out requests for book reviews. Sometimes multiple genres are needed to suit the situation, and part of whether you can do the work depends on your own skills in particular genres.

Cheryl worked with co-editor Drew Loewe to create a set of marketing materials for a book they wanted to promote: *Bad Ideas about Writing*. The primary audience for the book was people who teach writing, or want to know how writing is taught, but who don't have research backgrounds in writing studies. This made publicity tricky because it was an unfamiliar audience. But they also wanted to reach readers who were academics and who attended an annual conference on writing studies where they could showcase some printed materials at an exhibit booth. So Drew designed a flyer that could mimic a possible book cover (see **Fig. 3.9**), and they provided a single proof copy of the book for display at the booth. To publicize that these materials were available at the conference, Cheryl circulated a selfie holding the proofs on her social media accounts (see **Fig. 3.10**) where she knew thousands of potential readers would see it. Sure enough, these two methods of multimodal outreach garnered attention for the book with the academic audience.

But what should they have done to reach the nonacademic audience? What suggestions would you have made to them? Would you have circulated a video on Twitter? Designed an Instagram Story? Made a TikTok? Or are there other multimodal texts they could have made to promote the book?

What kind of project are *you* working on? How will you research the situation to understand the genres it will require? What genre(s) seem most likely to persuade the audience you want to reach?

Figure 3.9 The Cover Flyer for *Bad Ideas about Writing*

Drew Loewe

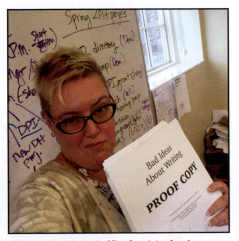

Figure 3.10 A Selfie for Marketing Purposes

Courtesy of Cheryl Ball

Genre Analysis: Analyzing the *What* and the *How*

Performing a genre analysis can pose the problem of COIK: Clear Only If Known—that is, how can a reader identify the genre of a text and relate it to other texts unless they are already familiar with that kind of genre to begin with? As teachers, we see this problem exhibited all the time when students call any printed form of a book a *novel* if they think it's read outside of an academic setting but call a book a *textbook* if it's any printed, long-form text read for a class. But they run into confusion when teachers mix genres, such as assigning a novel like Zadie Smith's *White Teeth* for a class but referring to it as a textbook. Texts can fall into multiple genres, or contain mixtures of genres, and conflating the genres of all printed, long-form books into either novels or textbooks—or just books—misses the nuances of these subgenres. A cookbook is not at all the same genre as a diary, which is again not at all the same genre as a biography. And those genres of books are totally different from self-help books, guides, or dictionaries, even though all of these examples are long-form, often-printed books.

And, yet, books are an easy example, relatively speaking, because they're so familiar. Most readers of *this* book (a guidebook, which is a subgenre of a textbook, for the record) will recognize it as a book, and maybe even a kind of textbook. Why? Because you recognize how its rhetorical and multimodal design elements—through words, layout, graphics, organizational structure, and so on—work together to form a whole, cohesive text. You've seen similar texts. You know that it is *not* a story in the narrative sense, so it's probably not a novel. And you are meant to learn explicit information from it. But how do you apply what you've implicitly learned about identifying genres, such as this textbook, to other kinds of multimodal texts?

Like a rhetorical analysis, which is meant to help readers and potential authors understand the audience, purpose, and context in which a text was designed (see Chapter 2), **genre analysis** is meant to help readers and potential authors examine how the container of that information allows the *what* (the content of your text) and the *how* (the form your text takes) to work together within specific rhetorical situations. In that way, genre analyses and rhetorical analyses work hand in hand; it isn't actually possible to separate what you want to say from how you will say it. Your topic and your design are closely connected, which is why this book is called *Writer/Designer*. You can't be just a writer or just a designer; you're always both. And it's more useful to interpret how and why a particular genre works

Figure 3.11 Panel from *Understanding Rhetoric*, by Elizabeth Losh, Jonathan Alexander, Kevin Cannon, and Zander Cannon

This panel talks about comics while using the genre conventions of a comic.

for a text if the reader knows the rhetorical situation in which the text is being used.

Analyzing Genre Conventions

Even if you're just posting an update to Twitter (**Fig. 3.12**), you have to consider what you will say, how you will say it given who will see it, the context (the time of day, the event about which you're posting, etc.), and the ways that Twitter allows you to post supplementary information, such as links or photos. Additionally, the design of Twitter's user interface restricts the choices you can make as you craft your tweet; for example, you can't post anything longer than 280 characters. This situation is both rhetorical, in which you have to persuade a specific audience within a specific context, and generic, in that your purpose must be enacted within the confines of Twitter's conventions, some of which include the real-time nature of posting, the 280-character limit, the use of hashtags, occasional textspeak ("smh") to suit your audience or fit the character limit, and the integration of multimedia, as necessary. All of those characteristic features of Twitter posts are **genre conventions**.

If you learn to analyze the genre conventions of a text, you can better understand its rhetorical situation and apply that analytical

Figure 3.12 Genre Conventions of Twitter

In this selection of tweets, Kristin employs genre conventions such as a funny but otherwise plain ol' tweet about her day (top); a much more serious retweet from José Cortez with an air quality map (middle); and a comment and a retweet of a text that includes an image, a hashtag, and shout-outs to specific Twitter users (bottom).

With permission of Jose M. Cortez and Julian Chambliss

skill to any kind of text you come across. You can also add more design choices to your rhetorical knowledge every time you compose a text for a new rhetorical situation.

For example, if you were to analyze breast cancer pamphlets, you would find that almost all of them feature a pink ribbon and a script-like font. These are genre conventions that authors and readers use to make meaning within a rhetorical situation because they are design elements that have become socially accepted as a metaphorical representation of breast cancer. It's important to analyze how conventions are used within texts because genre conventions are a good starting place when designing a similar text for a similar rhetorical situation. They help us understand what audiences expect from particular kinds of texts in particular kinds of situations. For example, if you're making a breast cancer awareness brochure, do you need to use the pink ribbon in order to be taken seriously? Or are there good reasons to break with this genre convention? As we saw with the figure of the lemons in Chapter 2 (see p. 40), just because a design element like the pink ribbon has become part of the social fabric of a particular genre and rhetorical situation doesn't mean that it's the only design element possible; sometimes changing that element can help a designer reach a whole new audience.

Questions for Genre Analysis

When analyzing genre, the following questions help you discover patterns that illuminate genre conventions across multiple sets of texts in a single genre:

- How is the text written and designed? How does a text convey its meaning? What modes and media does it predominantly use? Is it similar to other texts you've seen? How so?

- What multimodal elements do you notice, and how are they organized in the text? Do they create hierarchies of emphasis? Spatial relationships? Navigational choices appropriate to the situation?

- Does the text contain a combination of other genres (for example, an air-quality map in a tweet)? How does the mixture of genres work together to convey meaning?

- How might you define the genre (or subgenres) of the text? If it is a subgenre, what conventions are different from its main genre that make it seem different?

- What is the purpose of this particular genre in relation to this particular rhetorical situation? What does the genre expect from readers? What does it allow/ask readers to do?

⊙— Touchpoint: **Analyzing Musical Genres**

What are the conventions of songs that can be classified under the genres of rock, pop, jazz, classical, rap, EDM, or country? Some classical music, with its soothing stringed instruments or mellow piano solos, might help relax or calm us, while EDM's quick, pulsing beats might energize us enough to dance. Sites such as Google Play and Spotify categorize songs by musical genres and suggest certain playlists in genres depending on the listener's mood, which they can pick from using an interactive mood list that may also incorporate images (see **Fig. 3.13**). These tools—and our brains—rely on pattern recognition to classify musical genres. That pattern recognition is based on genre conventions. And while not every song within a particular genre uses the exact same conventions, being able to recognize the patterns can help us distinguish one song, and genre, from another.

Pick a song, any song—it may be your favorite song, your most hated song, the most popular song on the radio, the song you're listening to right now. What mood does it put you in? What patterns does it have? How is it structured? Are the answers to these questions related? Identify and consider other songs in the same genre: Do they make you feel the same way? Do they have similar patterns or structures? How would you answer the Questions for Genre Analysis from page 73 for your genre?

Figure 3.13 Spotify Playlists

Streaming services like Spotify help listeners choose a musical genre and song based on mood or activity.

Analyzing Multimodal Genres in Game Studies

Two Different Genres: The *What* versus the *How*

Let's look at two examples to see more clearly how genres are dependent on the connection of the *what* and the *how* and on the rhetorical situation. Here are two texts that discuss the topic of video games and learning:

1. A scholarly book called *What Video Games Have to Teach Us about Learning and Literacy* by James Paul Gee, in which the author, drawing on lots of other scholarly research, argues that video games help promote literacy because they offer complicated, interactive narratives that game players have to learn to navigate. (See **Fig. 3.14**.)

2. A prezi (an interactive, online, multimedia presentation application) called "Playing to Learn?" by Maria Andersen, in which she argues that using games in the classroom is an effective teaching tool because it engages students' brains in different ways and keeps them interested in learning tough topics (like math, which she teaches). (See **Fig. 3.15**.)

So the *what* is that these two scholar-teachers agree that games are good pedagogical tools. And they give lots of scholarly and popular examples as to why games are good for us. In making our own project, we could cite

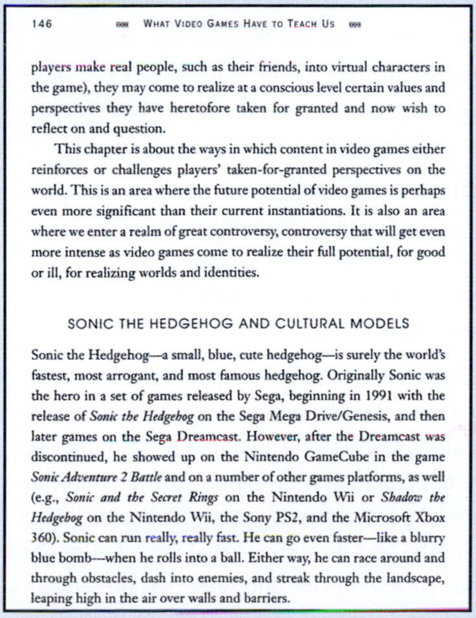

146   ∞   WHAT VIDEO GAMES HAVE TO TEACH US   ∞

players make real people, such as their friends, into virtual characters in the game), they may come to realize at a conscious level certain values and perspectives they have heretofore taken for granted and now wish to reflect on and question.

This chapter is about the ways in which content in video games either reinforces or challenges players' taken-for-granted perspectives on the world. This is an area where the future potential of video games is perhaps even more significant than their current instantiations. It is also an area where we enter a realm of great controversy, controversy that will get even more intense as video games come to realize their full potential, for good or ill, for realizing worlds and identities.

SONIC THE HEDGEHOG AND CULTURAL MODELS

Sonic the Hedgehog—a small, blue, cute hedgehog—is surely the world's fastest, most arrogant, and most famous hedgehog. Originally Sonic was the hero in a set of games released by Sega, beginning in 1991 with the release of *Sonic the Hedgehog* on the Sega Mega Drive/Genesis, and then later games on the Sega Dreamcast. However, after the Dreamcast was discontinued, he showed up on the Nintendo GameCube in the game *Sonic Adventure 2 Battle* and on a number of other games platforms, as well (e.g., *Sonic and the Secret Rings* on the Nintendo Wii or *Shadow the Hedgehog* on the Nintendo Wii, the Sony PS2, and the Microsoft Xbox 360). Sonic can run really, really fast. He can go even faster—like a blurry blue bomb—when he rolls into a ball. Either way, he can race around and through obstacles, dash into enemies, and streak through the landscape, leaping high in the air over walls and barriers.

Figure 3.14 A Page from James Paul Gee's *What Video Games Have to Teach Us about Learning and Literacy*

Looks like a book, eh?

Figure 3.15 "Playing to Learn?," Maria Andersen's Prezi about Using Games to Teach Effectively

Looks like a game, eh?

Maria Andersen, Prezi, Inc.

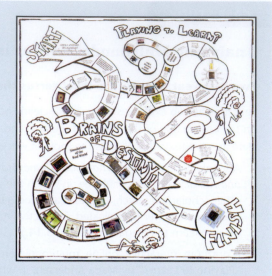

Write/Design Toolkit

Refer to "Citing Assets and Sources" on page 158 for more info on citation.

either of these texts to support our own argument about games. Citing sources is something you probably have some experience with already, so for now we want to focus on *how* these authors make their arguments.

On the one hand, Gee (pronounced like the letter G or "Gee whiz!") has written a scholarly book that relies on the genre's conventions (like prose, citations, and formal language) to connect with his audience. There are visual modes—a few tables—but the text consists mostly of words formatted in a way that we're used to seeing in scholarly (or even popular) books. That is to say, his book looks pretty much like every other book in that genre (see **Fig. 3.14**).

Andersen, on the other hand, has chosen to present the same topic using a much different design: a media-rich, interactive presentation on the website Prezi.com. She also includes citations and examples, just like Gee does, although hers are usually much more brief because of the design conventions afforded by the Prezi interface.

Write/Design Toolkit

See "Assessing Technological Affordances" on page 174 for more on the impact of technological choices on designing multimodal projects.

However, unlike Gee, Andersen makes her argument about how games promote learning by designing her text to *look like* a game (see **Fig. 3.15**), which adds visual, spatial, and gestural meaning to her linguistic text. Andersen doesn't have to present as much linear, written information as Gee does to get a similar point across because she has the visual, spatial, and gestural design of the text do some of that work better than the linguistic mode could do. Thus, *how* Gee and Andersen present their topics is as important as *what* they want readers to get from their texts.

Gee's and Andersen's works are different, despite their similar topics, because they are written for different audiences and purposes. Gee's purpose is to reach an audience of public readers who are interested in games and reading practices; he also wants to reach academics who study literacy and gaming. Andersen's purpose is to use the multimodal and interactive affordances of a prezi, which helps her create a gamelike experience, to persuade teachers that games can engage students' brains by keeping them interested in learning tough topics. One text is meant for solitary, in-depth reading, while the other could be presented to a group of people in a shorter amount of time. One text is not better than the other because they serve different rhetorical situations.

The Same Genre: Analyzing Conventions

Now, let's compare texts within the same genre: Andersen's gaming prezi with two other prezis about the same topic (see **Figs. 3.16** and **3.17**). We can use this exercise to figure out what genre conventions authors of prezis have come to use and have used successfully.

Prezi software is based on our genre knowledge of other presentation tools (like Keynote and PowerPoint, which are in turn based on our knowledge of poster presentations). However, Prezi is also significantly different from other presentation software in that it allows readers to create zooming and anima-tion features that are very difficult, if not impossible, to use in other presen-tation tools. For this reason, it is rare to run across a PowerPoint presentation

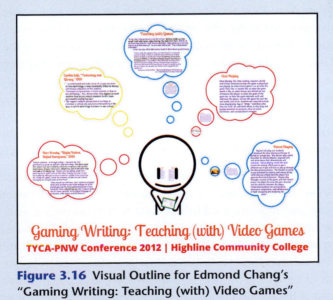

Figure 3.16 Visual Outline for Edmond Chang's "Gaming Writing: Teaching (with) Video Games"

Courtesy of Edmond Chang

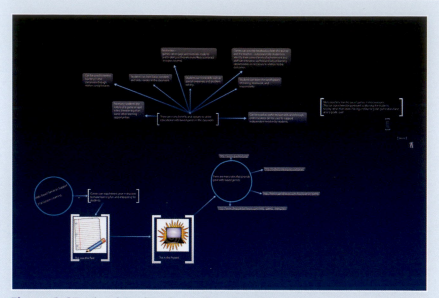

Figure 3.17 Visual Outline for William Maelia's "Using Web-Based Games to Support 21st Century Learning"
William Maelia, Prezi, Inc.

that you're expected to interpret without any help from the author (e.g., notes posted online from a class lecture are still intended to go *with* the face-to-face lecture), whereas with Prezi you are more likely to run across presentations that stand on their own. Thus, similarity across prezis becomes one possible genre convention, as noted in the table on page 79 (on the row titled "Does the text make sense on its own?"). We could list many more conventions in the table, but we'll leave it at these, just to give you an idea of how you might come up with your own comparative list. For example, based on the number of readers who have "liked" each of the prezis in the table, we might be able to judge the prezis' relative success, although such an evaluation doesn't do justice to some of the successful qualities within the two prezis that have few or zero likes so far. The more stand-alone the prezi is, the more successful it seems to be.

Of course, if you are required to create a presentation for your multimodal project and you know that the rhetorical situation requires you to deliver it personally, perhaps your presentation will still be successful even if your prezi doesn't stand alone. You just have to figure out *which* conventions are needed to make the text interesting and useful for your audience. For instance, the three prezis analyzed here use the standard linear navigation path, which allows readers to click on the right arrow to navigate to the next set of information, as opposed to readers skipping around or the authors placing information outside of the path for readers to discover on their own. The latter types of navigation would be more appropriate for readers to play with in a stand-alone piece than in a public presentation. The navigation path that your presentation uses is a design decision you have to make based on your rhetorical situation.

Prezi Genre Conventions

Prezis	Andersen's "Playing to Learn?"	Chang's "Gaming Writing: Teaching (with) Video Games"	Maelia's "Using Web-Based Games to Support 21st Century Learning"
URL (for reference)	http://prezi.com /rj_b-gw3u8xl/	http://prezi.com /ai6wnm0l_j1l/	http://prezi.com /yiknhf2wapi_/
Background color	White	White	Blue
Navigation	Left and right arrows	Left and right arrows	Left and right arrows
Use of words	Uses titles, quotes, and explanatory text	Uses titles, quotes, and explanatory text	Uses titles and explanatory text
Levels of zoom and rotation	Zooms in on key elements; rotation follows game board path	Zooms in on frame; no rotation	Mostly uses same level of zoom throughout (with a few variances); minimal rotation
Author	Bio and contact info in Prezi	Contact info in Prezi	No information in Prezi
Use of images	Images supplement the written text	Images convey an example	Very few images are used, and mostly for shock value
Path points	103	14	22
Does the text make sense on its own?	Yes	Yes	Yes
Use/purpose of navigational path	Path is designed around a background illustration that corresponds to the argument; great "bigger picture" view	Path revolves around central figure; "bigger picture" conveyed through thought bubbles	Path is based on mind-mapping concept, but not all nodes are related; some "bigger picture" purpose
Citations	Yes	Yes	No (but there is a resource list)
Number of reader likes	More than 2,200	< 10	0
Use of video/ animation	Yes (15)	No (0)	No (0)

What if the Genre Is Unclear?

When researching texts for your multimodal project, you may come across a text whose genre is unclear. If you don't know the genre of a text, remember that genres are created based on other genres, on shared social circumstances, and for rhetorical situations that authors are familiar with. So, if you don't know the genre, ask yourself what the text *reminds* you of. Then maybe ask a few of your friends, your supervisor, or your teacher the same question. It's likely that collectively you'll be able to identify a genre that most closely fits the kind you want to study further. Also, texts sometimes mash up multiple genres. For example, when social networking sites (like Twitter) were first created, they asked users to "microblog" in 140 characters or less (the original limit of tweets), whereas blog posts are typically much longer than that. The term *microblog* shows that when status updates were new, they were compared most closely in genre to blogs. So if you encounter a text whose genre is new to you, see what other genres the text relates to and consider studying those as well.

write/design! assignment

Analyzing Genre Conventions for Your Project

Now it's time for you to start working on your multimodal project, putting together your skills in rhetorical-multimodal-genre analysis. This step assumes that you have a project concept in mind—one that a teacher, client, or supervisor has provided or one that you have artistic freedom to create yourself. If you don't yet have a multimodal project in mind, you can use the example proposal from Chapter 4 or a project you've worked on in any of the Touchpoint activities, talk to your teacher or supervisor for ideas, or just pick your favorite kind of text to practice with.

1. Find and read/view/explore eight to ten texts across a range of media. They should all be on the same topic, as with "game studies" in the Case Study (pp. 75–79).

2. List the arguments, points, or key ideas those texts offer about your topic. This is the *what*. For instance, in the Case Study above, both Gee and Andersen focused on how teaching games improves students' learning. That's a key idea within the topic of games.

3. Next, list the multimodal design choices (think back to the list of modes in Chapter 1—linguistic, visual, aural, spatial, and gestural—and the design choices in Chapter 2—emphasis, contrast, organization, alignment, and proximity) that the texts use. This is the *how*.

4. Analyze the relationship between the *what* and the *how* (using rhetorical genre analysis—context, author, purpose, audience, and genre) and decide which texts seem the most successful given their rhetorical situations.

5. Identify which themes in those successful texts most inspire you to do further research. (If a key idea seems to be missing from the list you compiled in step 2, that might also be a good place to do more research.) Shorten your list of themes down to one or two ideas.

6. Pick one genre from those texts that you think best fulfills the author's purposes for that rhetorical situation. Do some research to find two or three more texts in that genre (they do not have to be on the same topic, although they might be). If several genres seem particularly appealing and successful, research them all.

7. Analyze the examples in this genre or genres and make a list or table of similarities and differences. These might relate to design choices such as layout, navigation, and multimodal elements, as well as to what each of those choices accomplishes within the text. You may also list rhetorical choices such as audience, purpose, context, historical period, and so on. Refer to Chapter 2 for a sampling of rhetorical and design choices that you might use. Also, see the Case Study on pages 75–79 for an example of how to create this table.

What design elements are similar? Do they look similar or function in a similar way across most of the examples? If so, you have a genre convention. Make a short list of all the conventions for that particular genre, which you should keep as a handy checklist when designing and assessing the quality of your own multimodal project in that same genre.

write/design! option: Infographics as Visual-Argument Genres

One interesting place to see multimodal rhetorics at work is in the increasingly common genre of infographics like the one on page 67. The multiple modes available for use in infographics give writer/designers a set of affordances with the potential to make information more appealing, accessible, and inviting to a larger audience through placing those ideas within a story.

A writer/designer creating an infographic has to make rhetorical and multimodal choices to best fit their audience, purpose, and context. One of the cardinal rules of an infographic is to keep it concise, stripping away everything except the essentials. At the same time, every element—from font style, size, and color to the use of photographs, charts, and graphs—has an impact on how an audience will make sense of information and respond to an infographic's message.

Begin by selecting a topic or issue of interest to you or that is suggested by your instructor. Search for and save at least five infographics on your topic. As you begin collecting your infographic examples, consider the following questions and be ready to discuss them with the rest of the class:

- Which infographic is your favorite and why? Which is your least favorite and why?
- Which infographic do you think is the most informative and why? Is it also the most persuasive one? Why, or why not?
- Which mode, media, and design choices seem to make the most sense for the subject and context? Are these used in the same way in all five examples, or do they work particularly well in just one?

Once you've chosen your topic and done a quick genre analysis of other infographics on the subject, it's time to start composing your own. Your

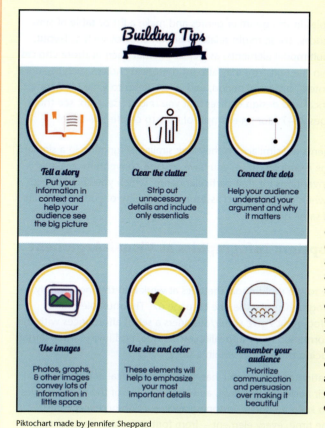

Piktochart made by Jennifer Sheppard

Figure 3.18 Visual Arguments Infographic

Infographic writer/designers have to balance ways of making their texts visually appealing and informative with the need to communicate ideas, data, and arguments clearly, concisely, and persuasively. This infographic is about creating infographics (meta!). The steps are clearly arranged, and visuals make the text appealing while conveying information through symbols. The text is kept to a minimum, with clear, directive titles ("Tell a story") and brief elaboration in a less emphatic font.

purpose is to condense and visualize your topic/research material, making it more comprehensible and persuasive for a broad audience.

While you can always create an infographic by hand, drawing on a large piece of paper, you might also want to do a first or final draft digitally. There are many free or low-cost options for creating your own infographic online. Sites such as Piktochart, Canva, Infogram, Easelly, or Visme have a set of free templates or the option to join with access to dozens more templates. Just make sure to check how these sites allow you to access your infographic after you create it, in case you need to send a copy to your teacher or client—not all allow you to download your text after you've made it. Alternatively, you can search online for infographic templates.

Write/Design Toolkit

See the Touch-point Activity "Creating a Sustainability Plan" on page 200 for guidance on making sure your work remains accessible and sustainable in the multimodal afterlife.

4

How Do You Start a Multimodal Project?

So far in this book, we have discussed what multimodal texts are, how they work rhetorically through design, and the role that genre plays in communicating an author's message to an audience. Since the point of this book is to help you become a multimodal writer/designer, we now want to offer a big-picture perspective of how authors begin the process of making multimodal projects.

As you gain expertise at writing/designing, the process becomes easier, and you might even be able to skip some of these steps (or work them out informally). These steps should not be taken as set in stone. They are guides for thinking through the composition process, not a rigid, lockstep method for getting things done.

This chapter provides an overview of the typical early stages of a multimodal composition process, including brainstorming and refining initial ideas, pitching those possibilities to others as a means of gaining feedback, researching, planning and articulating a more detailed proposal, and developing mode-appropriate drafts (e.g., storyboards, mock-ups, wireframes, and prototypes). We then demonstrate how that process can play out in more detail through a comprehensive Case Study. While the Case Study example is likely more complex than what you will be working on at this stage, we hope that showing you this process in full will help you determine how to proceed on your own multimodal projects, now and in the future. The Write/Design! assignment that concludes the chapter guides you through proposing a project of your own and drafting a realistic timeline. Chapter 5, "How Do You Design and Revise with Multiple Audiences?," will show you the rest of the process, from revision to finished product.

What Are You Supposed to Produce?

Persuasive texts are almost always written in response to some situation (what rhetoricians call an exigency). Sometimes the authors producing those texts are self-motivated to action, such as writing a letter to the editor of a newspaper about a local issue the author is passionate about. When they aren't self-motivated, projects are the result of someone else giving instructions to follow: a teacher giving an assignment, a supervisor delegating a task to an employee, a nonprofit group developing a website to share their work and recruit volunteers, an organization soliciting business through a social media campaign or an advertisement, an owner of a lost pet posting a flyer, and so on. Each of these projects presents a new rhetorical situation that requires analysis to determine the purpose and audience(s), as well as the genre needed to fulfill the stakeholders' expectations.

This is where the analytical skills you built up in Chapters 2 and 3 will be useful for designing your own multimodal project. Determining what you are supposed to produce, for whom, for reading/use in which genre, and by when are the first steps in figuring out how you will complete your multimodal project. Once you've arrived at some initial answers to these questions, you are ready to begin drafting your project. Just remember, even the best-laid plans need adjustments, so build in at least a little flexibility.

Brainstorming Your Project Ideas

A big part of designing is experimenting with ways of combining content and form. This means that there isn't one perfect way to begin and it's perfectly OK (and normal) for your first ideas to need refinement. Coming up with several ideas as you conceptualize your project is a good strategy because sometimes your first idea might be too literal or too broad in scope, or it just may not be what you want. Once you have a general idea of your overall project and purpose, you can experiment to flesh out some of the details about what works and what doesn't. While this trial-and-error process can often take a long time initially, it's good practice to analyze multiple modes in relation to one another, and doing so often helps you develop unexpected communication possibilities. Plus, the more you practice putting modes together and analyzing how they affect readers, the more quickly you'll be able to design your next multimodal project.

Begin by brainstorming some design ideas. Record them quickly. It's not about how well you can draw or write but rather about getting the ideas down in visual and spatial (not just linguistic) form. It's also important that you don't censor yourself or stop to judge your ideas at this stage. You can evaluate them later, because now is the time for generating possibilities.

As Rachel Fernandes' visual brainstorming examples illustrate in **Figure 4.1**, this part of the composing process isn't about

Figure 4.1 Rachel's Visual Design Brainstorming

Student Rachel Fernandes brainstorms and tests her visualizations by creating multiple iterations of her mock city council logo.

Rachel Fernandes

making things look perfect on the first try, but rather about visualizing and recording your initial ideas. We recommend you choose a brainstorming format that seems most comfortable and intuitive to you and then get started! You could draw simple stick figures, make flowcharts, use icons to represent certain kinds of content, use colored pencils, crayons, or different-colored sticky notes (Jenny's favorite) if color is a significant part of the visual design, or work with other "craft" materials that you feel comfortable playing with as you experiment. Your brainstorming doesn't need to be elaborate at this stage. Focus on speed and quantity of ideas, not quality. There will be time later to perfect them. And although some authors, like Rachel, are more adept at creating these visualizations on their computers, we find that most authors are better off using pen and paper because it's less of an initial commitment and provides a quicker way to brainstorm.

⦿— Touchpoint: **Multimodal Brainstorming**

Imagine that your intramural soccer club has asked you to design a flyer to recruit more players for the upcoming season that starts next semester. Your club has decided to post the flyer in the residence halls and the student fitness center to target students new to campus and those who already enjoy physical activity. It is particularly important to recruit women players, as the team needs to have a certain ratio of men to women to qualify for the league. Given this rhetorical situation, brainstorm some initial design ideas for the flyer. Consider the following questions as you work:

- Your genre has already been designated as a flyer, but what are the options and conventions within the genre that would best suit your needs (paper size and color, type of paper, layout, those little tear-away tags at the bottom so that your audience physically takes a copy of your club's contact information)?

- What basic information must be included (game and practice times, season duration, experience level, costs, field location, contact email or website link, etc.)?

- What design elements and participation perks can you emphasize to encourage students to join? What specific strategies will you use to recruit women players?

- What design constraints do you have to work with (team or school colors, logos, images, etc.)?

Pitching Your Project

Once you have done some brainstorming and reflected on the kind of project you plan to make, your next step is to refine those early ideas so that you can seek feedback from others and move forward with developing your initial draft. Since there is no single approach or kind of text that will work in all situations for all audiences, knowing how to perform rhetorical analyses and looking closely for genre conventions will help you figure out how to write or design any kind of text. However, it's also important to look for guidance and insight from others to see if there are alternative perspectives or approaches you need to incorporate. By explaining your early project ideas to your teacher, classmates, boss, client, or other stakeholders before you begin the bulk of your design work, you can be better assured that you're on the right track as you create a text for a particular rhetorical situation.

A **pitch** is a short and informal write-up or presentation that briefly conveys your initial project concept. It explains how the *what* (content) and the *how* (form) of your idea might come together in the final project. It's a means of convincing audience members who have some stake in what you are proposing that you understand the situation/issue, have an interesting and relevant plan for approaching it, and can successfully accomplish the project at hand. (Pitches are sometimes called elevator speeches, drawing on the idea of a writer who is on an elevator with a publisher and has only a few floors to convince the publisher to accept their book proposal.) Importantly, pitches can also be used as a way of getting feedback on the early concept and direction of your project *before* you have spent time developing it. Once you've gotten support or approval for an idea you've pitched, you can start fleshing out the form and content of the project in the recursive stages discussed later in this chapter.

Keep in mind that at this point you have not completed a lot of research into the topic or designs, so there will be room for change. This is the same basic process used in writing essays; you have an initial idea based on the assignment directions, but as you begin researching and writing on the topic, your focus will become more concrete, or it might change direction, or it might even take a completely different form.

A pitch (or a more formal proposal, discussed at the end of this chapter) can be especially valuable for writer/designers

of multimodal texts. That's because a change in topic or
a refinement in your argument might cause a significant
rethinking and reworking of the project's genre, design, and use
of multiple modalities — it's no longer as easy as cutting and
pasting words into a different order. You should expect and plan
for some level of contingency in your project idea as your work
progresses, but the more you can work out the kinks through a
pitch or proposal before drafting, the more efficient your efforts
will be.

Designing Your Pitch

Once you've brainstormed your ideas, it's time to put together a
pitch for your instructor, supervisor, peers, or other stakeholders.
(Note that sometimes you will create a pitch or a proposal, but not
both. While each is a useful kind of planning tool, these texts can
also differ in timing, scope, audience, research, and level of detail.)
When planning your pitch, make sure you address the following
details about your project:

- What is the rhetorical situation for your multimodal *project* (as
  opposed to your pitch)?

- What is your topic?

- What genre will you use for your project?

- How will you design your project in relation to your topic?
  How is the design appropriate to your project's rhetorical
  situation? Providing drawings from a multimodal brainstorm session (like the ones you may have done for the
  Multimodal Brainstorming Touchpoint on p. 87) might be
  useful here.

- What do you need to know or learn so that you can complete your project? In other words, how do you convince
  your instructor, stakeholders, or other audience members
  that you will be able to complete this project in the time
  frame given?

You'll also need to think about designing the *pitch* itself:

- What is the rhetorical situation of your pitch? (Who are you
  pitching to and why?)

- What genre of pitch does the rhetorical situation require (live
  presentation, stand-alone presentation, paper handouts, a

formal written proposal)? What genre conventions are necessary in your pitch?

- How will you convey your topic to your pitch audience? How much do they need to know at this point in the project, and what will you tell them to hook their interest? (How much more research do you need to do?)

- Are there other requirements for your pitch, such as a time limit, a specific technology, or a dress code?

Figure 4.2 illustrates how one student used these guidelines to pitch her project for improving access to lactation rooms on campus. After brainstorming and then writing up her ideas, Sarah pitched her project to her instructor and classmates, who then asked questions and offered suggestions to refine her plans.

◎— Touchpoint: Putting a Project Pitch into Action

Consider a multimodal project you've seen or are working on. Or, if you aren't currently working on a project, imagine you're developing a novel, movie, or video game and you need to pitch it to a publisher or studio (stakeholders) so that they invest in your project. Using the questions for designing your pitch on pages 89–90 as a guide, consider the elements you need to address as you write/design your pitch.

- What is the rhetorical situation and genre for the project?

- What is your topic, and what research do you need to do?

- How will you design your pitch? You could use a simple pitch like Sarah did (see **Fig. 4.2**), or you might decide to use another medium or genre such as a video or slide deck pitch.

Once you have considered these questions, create your pitch! Then practice it with your coworkers, classmates, or friends before pitching it to your stakeholders.

Improving Access to Lactation Rooms on Campus

Sarita

My idea for the project is to integrate my internship at the Women's Resource Center with advocacy for expanded lactation room locations on campus. This is a critical issue because with 35,000 students at this university, there is a large population of students, faculty, and staff who are moms and very few resources are provided to support their success. Right now, there are only three lactation rooms on campus: one in the Women's Resource Center, one in the library, and one inside of the student union. There are currently about 30 women who are actively involved in the lactation program, but there is a lack of both space and ease of access. All lactation room users have to schedule an appointment in advance to take care of their needs. This is a problem because, biologically, women may need to express milk at varying times that can't be planned in advance. In addition to the scheduling issues, the physical locations of the existing rooms and the large geographic footprint of our campus can force users to walk 15-20 minutes one-way to access one of the rooms. This can obviously negatively affect the work, retention, and academic/professional success of the mothers of our campus community.

> **35,000** students on campus
>
> **3** lactation rooms

My project will advocate for three primary changes.

1 **More Rooms**
The program needs to obtain additional lactation room spaces across campus so that they are more easily accessible.

2 **Flexible Scheduling**
A more flexible scheduling system should be developed so that moms can find an available room on an as-needed basis.

3 **Improved Equipment**
All new and existing lactation rooms should be equipped with necessary items (breast pumps, wipes, etc.) needed by lactating mothers.

In order to achieve this plan, I propose to work closely with the coordinator at the Women's Resource Center to create a proposal and presentation to advocate for more rooms and supplies. My target audience for this project will be the Associated Students' student organization funding committee. The genre I plan to use is a slide presentation that includes cost charts, student population graphs, lactation room layouts, and other relevant images.

Figure 4.2 A Student Pitch

Sarita Tanori/Jennifer Sheppard

CASE STUDY

Pitching an App for the National Gallery

In this Case Study, we present a series of documents from a multimodal project to show how the authors moved from researching, **brainstorming,** and **conceptualizing** their design idea to **proposing, drafting,** and **prototyping.** This case study also shows how authors used the **feedback loop** to pitch the project and make adjustments based on feedback to better fit the client's rhetorical situation. Although this Case Study is probably more complicated than what you will be writing/designing at this stage, we hope that showing you this process in full will help you make conscious and productive decisions about how to proceed on your own multimodal project. Some parts of the analysis provided here (particularly in the Drafting and Designing a Prototype section) were adapted from the project documents, courtesy of Sarah Lowe, who was one of the instructors on this project.

The Rhetorical Situation

The project began when the Norwegian National Museum (NNM) (audience; stakeholder) published a solicitation (or call for ideas), asking designers (authors) to create activities (text) that would bring more museum patrons, especially families (primary audience), into some of their prominent, but less-visited, collections (purpose). As part of a joint US–Norwegian program in Museum Interaction Studies, two professors, Sarah Lowe from the University of Tennessee at Knoxville and Palmyre Pierroux from the University of Oslo, along with their respective graphic design and education students (**Fig. 4.3**), collaborated with the National Gallery in Oslo to pitch a set of interactive games, apps, and other activities (genre). In this Case Study, we present one student group's project, a game-like mobile app (genre) called Tales. The writer/designers on the team included Sofie Bastiansen, Kiernan Bensey, Mette Bergsund, August Houston, Heather McNamara, Alex Raykowitz, and Suzanne Rye (authors).

In order to complete this project, the team had to

- Read the solicitation and understand the museum's project requirements (rhetorical situation; genre).

Figure 4.3 Designers (Left to Right): Kiernen Bensey, Alex Raykowitz, August Houston, Heather McNamara.

In addition to the authors and faculty listed previously, the project team included stakeholders Per Bakke and Anne Qvale from the National Museum of Art, Architecture and Design in Oslo, Norway.

Courtesy of Sarah Lowe, University of Tennessee School of Design. Designers, left to right: Kiernen Bensey, Alex Raykowitz, August Houston, Heather McNamara

- Research the National Gallery to get a sense of the space and to choose which lesser-known collection they wanted to focus on. The solicitation specified that the project could not focus on rooms with well-recognized art, such as the Edvard Munch exhibit with his famous painting, *The Scream* (rhetorical situation).

- Analyze the rhetorical situation of their chosen exhibit—in this case, using the content from the Collection Highlights exhibit in the National Gallery (context) to create a game (purpose) for multigenerational families (audience).

- Figure out the challenges, constraints, and other requirements that would be necessary to work with and against when designing their project (modes; affordances; design elements; audience; purpose; context).

- Ensure that the project met all the stakeholders' requirements, including primary audiences (families visiting the museum), secondary audiences (museum staff), and tertiary audiences (museum curators, designers, and investors) (rhetorical situation; genre; audience).

Researching the Rhetorical Situation to Write the Proposal

The group researched these aspects of the assignment by analyzing the rhetorical situation; studying the museum, its layout, exhibits, and mission documents; talking with staff; and reading scholarly research about game theory and learning. With all of this information in mind, they brainstormed multimodal possibilities that would fit all of the project criteria. Following this work, they wrote up much of this research into a **design brief (Fig. 4.4)**, a **proposal** genre used in the design field to spell out the research, planning, and design concepts of a multimodal project to persuade a client, audience, or other stakeholders that their proposed idea will accomplish the project's goals and is the best choice among a variety of options.

The Tales project team's design brief showcased their proposed project—a scavenger-hunt app—and demonstrated how this would be the best genre and approach to engage families with children, the target audience outlined in the NNM's solicitation. This design brief provided a summary of the research into the who, what, when, where, why, and how that the project team completed in order to create a text that would suit the NNM's rhetorical situation. The design brief itself is multimodal and designed to help the stakeholders (instructors, client, and audience) understand and visualize the project.

Each section of the design brief plays a necessary role in pitching the project, and we've included pieces of it here to help you see how the Tales team navigated all the elements we've covered in the previous chapters (rhetorical situation, design elements, modes, affordances, genre, etc.). The screenshots presented in the Case Study do not represent a real app. As we've discussed, designers commonly make sketches, mock-ups, and even videos of static objects and animate them so that they don't have to create a cumbersome, expensive prototype in the actual technology or medium of the final project before key details and the overall approach are approved by stakeholders. That's what the Tales team did here for the project proposed in their design brief, prototype, and pitch presentation. (For more information about writing project **proposals** and **reports**, see pp. 105–6 at the end of this chapter as well as Chapter 5, "Reporting on Your Project," pp. 141–42.)

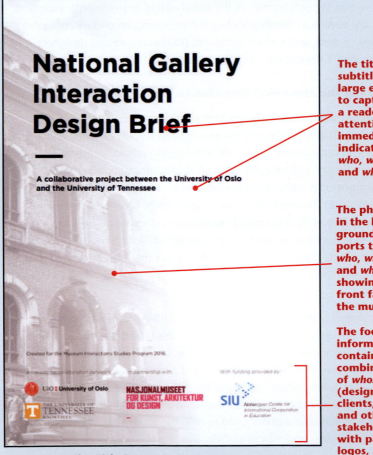

National Gallery Interaction Design Brief

—

A collaborative project between the University of Oslo and the University of Tennessee

Created for the Museum Interactions Studies Program 2016.

A collaboration between   in partnership with   With funding provided by

UiO : University of Oslo
THE UNIVERSITY OF TENNESSEE KNOXVILLE
NASJONALMUSEET FOR KUNST, ARKITEKTUR OG DESIGN
SIU Norwegian Centre for International Cooperation in Education

The title and subtitle are large enough to capture a reader's attention and immediately indicate the *who, what,* and *where.*

The photo in the background supports the *who, what,* and *where,* by showing the front façade of the museum.

The footer information contains a combination of *whos* (designers, clients, and other stakeholders), with partner logos, and *when* (2016).

Figure 4.4 **The Title Page**
Courtesy of Sarah Lowe, University of Tennessee School of Design

Justification of Project

The first three sections of the proposal—Needs Analysis, Literature Review, and Competitive Analysis (**Fig. 4.5**)—provide background research summarizing the why, what, and how.

- *Needs Analysis* (**Rhetorical Analysis**): This focuses on the fundamentals of audience, purpose, and context (see Chapter 1). For instance, here's a list of the subheads within the team's Needs Analysis that indicate the individual needs the project team identified:

  - **Project Partner:** Who is the National Museum? (audience; context)

  - **Content Scope:** What exhibits would the game feature and why? (purpose)

Competitive Analysis
Collection Highlights

ArtLens App (Gallery One)

The ArtLens app was designed for the Gallery One Art Exhibit within the Cleveland Museum of Art. This app allows you to experience the gallery space both within the museum and while at home, helping you to create a more personalized experience. At home, you are able to sort through the museum's gallery and view each piece as if you were there. When you are actually visiting the museum, you are able to walk around with the app through premade tours or simply scan them in order to see more information about each piece. You can then send your favorite pieces to the museum's Collection Wall that showcases images of the shared pieces.

Relevance:

An important aspect of this app is that it can exist beyond the walls of the museum, but in order to use it to its full potential, one must be within the space. It is important that our game be relevant within the space, but it may contain an aspect that can live outside of the museum.

12

Figure 4.5 The Competitive Analysis

This layout is typical in a report, which tends to privilege the use of images and summarized content that readers can quickly skim for meaning.

The image is emphasized according to its page placement and size because the visual design of the games are important to highlight in a competitive analysis.

A brief description fits into the remaining page length, with an informational header (the name of the app).

An even briefer paragraph indicates the relevance of analyzing this app.

- **Audience:** What are families' needs and interests? (audience)

- **Needs:** Why does the museum need to engage this audience? (purpose)

- **Project Challenge:** What problem will our team solve? (purpose)

- **Value:** What is the value of the outcome for the audience? (purpose)

- **Stakeholders:** Who will be involved in the outcome? (audience; context)

The needs analysis is similar to the background research you might include in a proposal for a project that has yet to be completed.

- *Literature Review* **(Research):** This section discusses the project's purpose in relation to previous research. For the Tales app, the team positioned their idea in conversation with research about using interactive games in learning environments. Literature reviews lend credibility **(ethos)** to your plans and help ensure that you aren't misunderstanding the rhetorical needs of a particular situation, or worse, reinventing the wheel. They also help show readers that you've researched what else has been done or written about and how your plans build on these previous ideas. In their lit review, the Tales team cited educational theory and other research to argue that interacting with artwork through a game will give museum visitors greater insight into and appreciation of the pieces they engage with, helping to support the team's and the NNM's goals.

- *Competitive Analysis* **(Genre Analysis):** This section compares the proposed project's look, function, and genre to projects that have already been designed for similar rhetorical situations to evaluate what has worked, what hasn't, and what can be adapted or improved upon. (For more on genre analysis, see Chapter 3, pp. 70–79.) The Tales team reviewed five art apps similar to (or in competition with) the one they wanted to create, summarizing the relevant research that pinpoints the goal of their project: Each competitor's product "involves interaction between the technology or game and the audience making them more engaging . . . which, according to research, is how learning occurs" (17).

Project Description

Based on the research they had conducted, the design team **brainstormed** ideas for this game-based app and settled on a scavenger-hunt genre that revolved around Redd, a red fox, who would help family members learn more about the artwork in the Collection Highlights section of the museum. Redd would ask them to work together to find clues that would help them

Figure 4.6 Redd

The main character in the Tales app.

Courtesy of Sarah Lowe

solve the puzzle he presented. In choosing Redd, the team drew on local culture and the fact that foxes are curious scavengers, following trails and digging up clues. Thus, Redd's character is a metaphorical embodiment of the game's purpose. One of the team members, a graphic design student, drew a version of Redd that they could use to think about how the game might proceed (see **Fig. 4.6**).

The family works together to help Redd find all the objects he needs to overcome stage fright and sing and dance at the King's Banquet. Each family member uses a different set of age-appropriate questions in the app to locate the artwork. Once found, players get additional information through questions and facts about the artwork, and they are rewarded with a specific item from the painting that Redd needs. For example, upon successfully finding Pablo Picasso's painting *Guitare*, an abstract representation of a guitar, the family learns more about abstraction in art as a method for self-expression, then they receive the guitar that Redd will need when he performs for the King. The seek-and-find activity continues through several stops in the gallery, concluding with an animation of Redd performing at the King's Banquet.

Drafting and Designing the Prototype

To **draft** their project, the Tales app team drew some sketches on paper first, created a digital drawing of Redd that they could more easily add facial features and stances to, created a mock-up of the app interface in an image-manipulation program like Photoshop or Illustrator, and then placed those images onto pictures of smartphones to make it seem as if they had already designed the app (see **Figs. 4.7** and **4.8**).

Write/Design Toolkit

For more guidance on creating prototypes, see "Prototyping for Static Texts" (p. 180).

Figure 4.7 **The Game Begins**

The fox's tail on the app's start screen points to the title of the game, Tales, which hearkens both to the tail of the fox and the narrative tale that the game provides. Each family member syncs their device to the code on the card, provided at the entrance to the museum exhibit. This initiates the game.

Courtesy of Sarah Lowe

In **Figure 4.8**, notice the repetition of color, design elements (Redd, the speech bubble, the "Found it!" button, navigational aids, etc.), and layout across the four screens. This design choice makes the different age-appropriate versions of the game feel like part of a single experience. The family plays as a team, with each of their player names at the top of each phone—but each player has a different set of clues appropriate for their age level. This design choice is based on the educational research the team has conducted on games and learning.

Creating the Stakeholder Pitch

Earlier in the chapter (see pp. 88–91), we discussed how a **pitch** can be used to help audiences understand the what, why, and how of your initial project ideas. These pitches are often brief and leave lots of room for change in the project conception after getting feedback and doing more research, and often they occur before the formal proposal that presents research and justification for your project. But sometimes pitches, as in this case, are more like formal presentations, where you have a fairly fleshed-out version, including a prototype, of the actual project. In all pitches, your

Figure 4.8 The Family Players
Courtesy of Sarah Lowe

primary purpose is to persuade. You are trying to convince your audience of the value and relevance of your project ideas and why they should approve yours or select it over others.

With the design brief and prototype complete, the Tales team presented a very detailed pitch of the project to a set of stakeholders, which included their instructors and external design critics who could give them feedback before they gave their final presentation to the museum. In designing their pitch, the team had to consider how to present the full rhetorical situation of the museum project as well as what the internal and external critics might need to know, especially since some of those in the audience (like Cheryl) were hearing about the project for the first time. The entire thirty-minute presentation was fifty-five slides, with each slide having no more than a sentence or two of content or an image or series of related images.

One of the design team members started the presentation by immediately showcasing the purpose of the project with a slideshow designed to echo the design of the app prototype (see **Fig. 4.9**). To provide background on the project, they had to tell the audience, in brief, why they chose to do the project this way. They drew from the research in their design brief proposal to create slides that had short bits of written content, summarizing the longer analytical sections (see **Fig. 4.10**).

Figure 4.9 Pitch Title Slide
Courtesy of Sarah Lowe

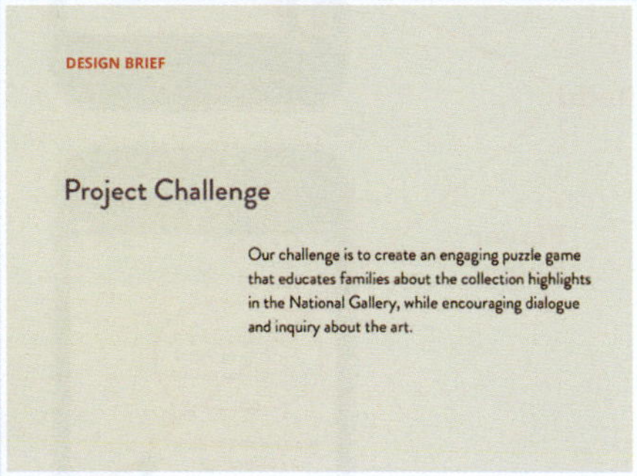

Figure 4.10 Project Purpose and Summary
Courtesy of Sarah Lowe

Next, the bulk of the presentation walked the audience through how the game would work for players—from the moment they entered the museum exhibit to the conclusion of playing the app—a segment of the presentation that took thirty-nine slides. Sample slides walked audiences through the registration process, gameplay description, summary of the remaining four quests, and the conclusion screen (see **Fig. 4.11**).

The presentation concluded with three slides reaffirming the value of this app in relation to a family's goals for playing and the museum's goals to increase family interaction with lesser-known works of art. The summary in the pitch presentation and the design brief or proposal helped remind stakeholders that it wasn't just a cool game but also a learning tool that met the objectives and outcomes they had desired. The team even went one step further in their verbal statement of values by suggesting that Redd the fox could be used as a branding tool, not just for this exhibit and app but for the museum as a whole, thus providing a larger potential impact for the clients than originally anticipated (which clients usually appreciate).

Individual players' registration screens.

Redd receives a gift—the pear—based on the artwork.

Game play is summarized visually and explained to audiences verbally.

Redd has received all their performance gifts.

Figure 4.11 Sample Slides from the Tales Pitch

Courtesy of Sarah Lowe

The Feedback Loop

One of the reasons we wanted to use Tales as an extended case study for this book is because the project team did an excellent job brainstorming, researching, and pitching their ideas to stakeholders. In the feedback loop, there was very little critical feedback requiring the team to change anything substantial in their design or their final presentation to the museum. In addition, stakeholders found the fox compelling and likable, and we (as authors of *Writer/Designer*) knew that the way the team had presented Redd and the Tales prototype would recreate well in a printed book. So, we wanted to offer you a collaborative, student-based example that could be achieved by writer/designers who don't specialize in graphic design. Sure, Redd is pretty fancy, and we can't draw that well ourselves, but as a model—and perhaps with a little help from other collaborators who will make your work stronger—you can work towards this type of pitch and project.

Designing for Your Primary Audience

As the Case Study in this chapter shows, one team worked to meet the needs of their primary audience: family members visiting a museum together. Only by effectively analyzing the rhetorical situation of the museum's call for proposals—thereby understanding the main context, purpose, and audience of the client's project—could the team propose to build the right app for the primary audience. Determining the details of who will see, hear, and use your project, either as part of pitching your project and writing your proposal or as part of the asset-gathering stages, will make your project more focused and your design tactics more precise.

Write/Design Toolkit

Details for gathering and tracking assets are discussed in more detail in "Collecting Assets" (p. 146).

Drafting to Stakeholder Expectations

Once you have pitched your ideas and gotten feedback and approval from your target audience (or other stakeholders), it's time to start the drafting process. At this stage, your work will likely include conducting research on your project's issue or topic, outlining your project's structure, and getting your rough ideas into physical form on paper, screen, or other modality.

Drafting is a recursive process. That means that you will continually make new content and then work to revise it to better suit your audience, purpose, and genre, which may then cause you to do more research, and so on. Depending on which genre you are composing, drafting might mean producing a different kind of text at various stages of the drafting process: from sketches (like in **Fig. 4.12**) or brainstorming notes; to pitches and proposals; to initial drafts,

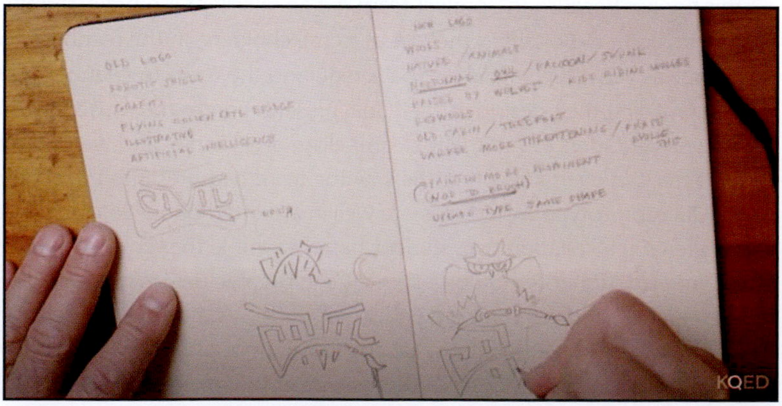

Figure 4.12 Brainstorming Sketches and Notes for a New Logo

storyboards, and scripts; to rough cuts, mock-ups, and alpha versions; to polished rough drafts such as prototypes or models.

Which term you use depends on what medium you're working in: the terms *rough cut*, *storyboard*, and *script* tend to be used with timeline-based projects such as videos or audio texts.

These forms of drafts allow you to plot out the linear order of content and what it will contain. In contrast, *prototype*, *wireframe*, *alpha version*, and *mock-up* are drafting terms typically used with code-based projects such as websites, apps, and software programs. As the Case Study shows, mock-ups and prototypes are often visual representations of how a project will look, but they don't yet contain any functionality to make them work. Further, keep in mind that different types of drafts are used for different purposes, with earlier options usually reserved for helping an author get their thoughts together on a project and later versions used for feedback from colleagues, clients, and occasionally target audiences themselves to fine-tune the final version.

Part Two of *Writer/Designer* provides an in-depth look at each of these forms of drafting, depending on what your composing needs are, so be sure to see these sections to select a genre appropriate for drafting your multimodal text:

- Outlines (p. 181)
- Sketches (pp. 181–83)
- Models (pp. 183–84)
- Wireframes (pp. 184–86)
- Mock-Ups (pp. 186–88)
- Storyboards (pp. 188–91)
- Scripts (pp. 191–92)
- Rough Cuts (pp. 192–94)

> **Write/Design Toolkit**
>
> For more examples on designing drafts for specific types of projects, see "Drafting Your Project: Static, Dynamic, and Timeline-Based Texts" (p. 178).

Touchpoint: Choosing a Draft Genre

After reading the information in this Drafting to Stakeholder Expectations section, visit the detailed drafting sections in Chapter 7, pages 178–80. Consider a project you are working on, the rhetorical situation, and your goals. Which genre is the right one for your project draft? Why is it the best choice?

Choose one and begin drafting your project!

Using the Feedback Loop

Authors rarely work in a vacuum with no feedback from an instructor, classmates/colleagues, supervisor, or other stakeholder, and writing/designing multimodal projects is no exception. When you draft a multimodal project for an audience, it's a good idea to solicit feedback from them that you can incorporate into your text. The **feedback loop** (see **Fig. 4.13**) is a method for checking your work with your stakeholders (see also the Chapter 5 sections on peer review on pp. 118–24). Feedback can happen throughout the process and often results in multiple revisions. This process is rarely linear and is often referred to as a loop. That is, you share your project, receive feedback, make revisions and move forward, and then receive more feedback, continuing on until you and/or the stakeholders (ideally both!) are satisfied.

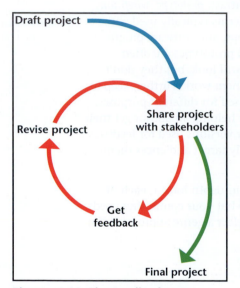

Figure 4.13 The Feedback Loop

You can also participate in others' feedback loops: Your fellow students or colleagues will often ask you to give them feedback on their early work. Providing productive feedback to others not only helps them but also strengthens your own critical skills and might even trigger ideas for your own work.

Besides classroom peer review, you may be familiar with other names for the feedback loop process, such as *workshopping* or *usability testing*. Typically, workshops are a part of the process that happens within a writing class and are a valuable part of the writing, design, and revision process. But since this book focuses on both real-world and classroom projects, our feedback loop is similar to usability testing, a term you hear in technical communication and other professional circles. Usability testing asks real users—those people who make up the target audience of your project—to perform certain tasks with your materials and report on their experiences. Since we suspect that users of this book are somewhere between the writing classroom and the professional world (if not in both), we use *feedback loop* as a compromise.

Finding out what your audience sees at this stage will forecast whether your design draft will successfully match what they want, need, and expect from the finished project. If your current plan isn't working, the feedback you receive should help you make changes to the draft and present it again until the draft is on the right track for its rhetorical situation. You don't want to progress too far along in composing the full project itself if you're not sure it will suit the rhetorical situation. It's *much* easier to change a mock-up, storyboard, or other early draft than to change a finished multimodal project, so take advantage of your feedback loop.

⦿— Touchpoint: Anticipating Feedback from Different Audiences

Feedback comes at multiple stages in the composing process—after designing a pitch, creating a draft, presenting a formal proposal, or sometimes anywhere along that windy path.

> **Write/Design Toolkit**
>
> For tips on presenting your rough draft to stakeholders, see "Getting Feedback on Your Rough Drafts" (p. 194).

It's important to keep track of who your audience or stakeholders are and how they respond or buy in to your project. At this point in your drafting, take a moment to consider whether you have adequately attended to all possible audiences for your project. You likely have a primary audience in mind, but what about audiences that don't immediately come to mind? Sometimes humans live in a bubble of who they know and who they have access to, which limits our interactions and knowledge of how other people, from different backgrounds, races, genders, cultures, abilities, and so on, might perceive or interact with a text. From the beginning of your planning stages, consider how to adjust your research, pitch, or draft to include people who might not immediately come to mind as potential users of your project.

write/design! assignment

Proposing to Get It All Done

This chapter's Case Study offered an inside look at a type of proposal called a design brief. Like most proposals, this one was used to document a project plan and to make a case for the strength and relevance of what the writer/designers intended to do. Proposals offer the opportunity to get feedback and to gain approval for moving forward with a project. Putting together your proposal will also be helpful as you design and build your project; it's a chance to make sure that you have a solid plan, that you have all the materials you'll need, that you know how to use the tools you want to use (or have a good plan for learning how to use them), and that you have a realistic schedule for getting everything done.

You can use or adapt the outline of the design brief presented in the Case Study to help write your proposal. Or here are some additional section headings and content ideas that will help convince your instructor, audience, or other stakeholders you are ready to embark on this project:

- **Abstract.** Give a brief overview of what your project is about, how you will approach it, and what genre you will use to fit the rhetorical situation.

- **Justification.** Discuss why your proposed design is appropriate and effective for making your argument. (Knowing your genre and its conventions will be helpful here; see Chapter 3, pp. 60–64.) This justification might also include analyses you have completed of similar genres and texts for this audience. (As shown in the design brief Case Study, this section is sometimes called a "literature review" or "competitive analysis.")

Write/Design Toolkit

See "Working with Technologies" (p. 169) for more on using different types of media and technology for your drafts and final texts.

- **Project description.** Fully describe your project concept and explain in detail what the rhetorical situation, genre, and audience will be. How will you design the project (including specific design elements, if known) to support your argument? Why do you need to use certain media, modes, or technologies to create a project that is useful to your particular audience?

- **Roles and responsibilities.** If you're working with a group, identify which group members are responsible for which project activities. If you have a group contract, consider attaching it to the proposal. (See Chapter 5, "Designing with Your Collaborators," pp. 109–15, for more info on working collaboratively.)

- **Timeline.** Give a detailed work plan of how and when you will complete all the project's components. (See the write/design! option assignment at the end of this chapter for more details on creating project timelines.) Make sure to include a breakdown of your tasks at each stage:
  - doing further research
  - collecting, editing, and documenting assets
  - preparing a draft
  - getting feedback on your final draft
  - revising
  - delivering your project

write/design! option: Project Timeline

You can create timelines for any project, from an essay to an app design. Working backwards from your project's final due date, figure out how long each stage of development will take and make a plan. Be sure to build in time for getting feedback and revising. Collecting assets, building a prototype, and making changes to content in multimodal projects often takes longer than an author has planned for, whether it is because equipment becomes unavailable or because deadlines for other projects and meetings interrupt the author's work. It's not unusual to have to repeatedly revisit a project timeline to make adjustments for different obstacles and constraints, but creating a timeline now can help avoid a crisis later.

As you work out your timeline, consider the following issues:

- **Stages:** What are the major milestones you need to accomplish and in what order?
- **Logistics:** Are there any logistics you need to keep in mind as you proceed, such as computer lab hours, instructional technology checkout limits, spring break, other class commitments, travel, or the like?
- **Collaborators and responsibilities:** Since multimodal projects often require collaboration, it's important to establish who will be responsible for completing what and by when.
- **Contingency plans:** What will happen if your process gets off schedule? What if a team member disappears? Have you built in any flex time? How will you adjust?

Although you can make a simple table in word processing or spreadsheet software to map out your timeline (like the one shown in **Fig. 4.14**), there are also a number of free online tools to create timelines visually. A Gantt chart (**Fig. 4.15** on p. 108) is a horizontal bar chart that illustrates the length of time key stages of a project will take, who will be responsible, and how those deadlines align with other activities in the development process.

Task	Project Dates					
	4/11	4/18	4/21	4/25	4/28	5/2
Discuss preliminary topic	All	All				
Complete proposal		A B C				
Complete timeline		B				
Begin research		All				
Complete research memo		C				
Team meeting with professor			All			
Ongoing research		All	All	All		
Draft report			A	A		
Edit and embedded images					B	
Workshop draft					A	
Revise report						C
Prepare presentation						B
Final revision and editing of report						All
Submit report						All
Deliver final presentation						All

A = Alice   B = Brett   C = Carol

Figure 4.14 A Simple Timeline Created in a Table or Spreadsheet

Courtesy of Jennifer Sheppard

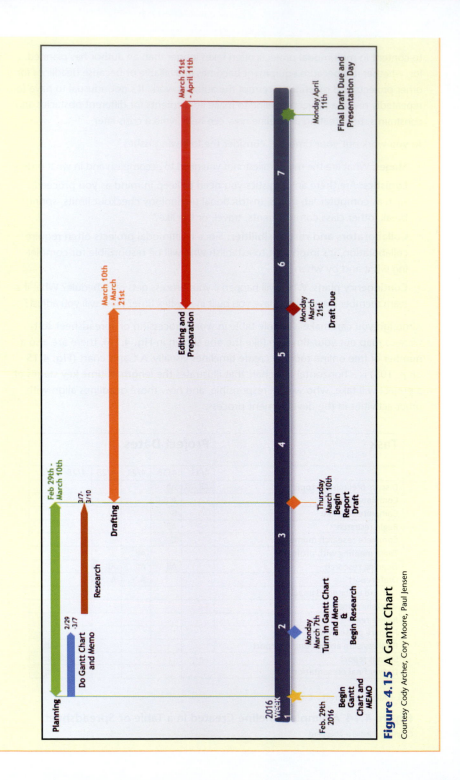

Figure 4.15 A Gantt Chart

Courtesy Cody Archer, Cory Moore, Paul Jensen

How Do You Design and Revise with Multiple Audiences?

5

In Chapter 2, we discussed the various audiences that multimodal projects can have, including primary audiences, such as readers and users, as well as secondary audiences, such as teachers, colleagues, and other stakeholders like clients, funding agencies, and others. Then, in Chapter 4, we showed you how one project team built the Tales app by considering their multiple audiences and getting feedback from some of them during the drafting process. This chapter takes you deep into that collaborative drafting process and the feedback loop with primary and secondary audiences of your own multimodal project. We start with collaborators because they are your project team and closest to you, but we also discuss what it's like to work on a multimodal project by yourself, which your project may call for. The second half of the chapter offers techniques for critiquing your multimodal work during the design process and creating a revision and delivery plan for your project.

Designing with Your Collaborators

Every reader of this book has likely had some kind of experience working with a group, and it's equally likely that not every collaborative experience has been a good one. As teachers and writer/designers, the three of us have certainly seen our fair share of collaborative projects go awry, whether because of conflict over the topic or direction of a project, personal disagreements among members of a group, or group members who don't contribute what they're supposed to. We also know firsthand, from the experience of writing this book together, that collaborating is hard work, especially when you have people who can't meet together in the same place and who have strong opinions on the way things should be done. However, this book wouldn't have been the same if any one of us had written it alone.

Collaborating with others, especially on multimodal projects, does have big benefits, but it can present complications that are better worked through from the beginning of a project. For instance, in the first edition of this textbook, we tried to use an early version of

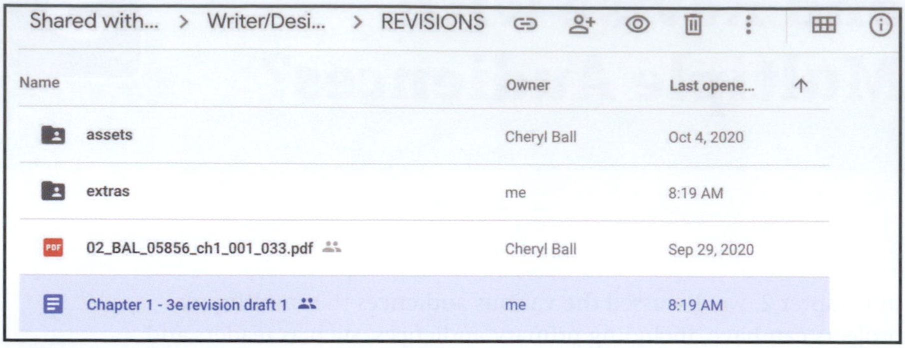

Name	Owner	Last opene... ↑
assets	Cheryl Ball	Oct 4, 2020
extras	me	8:19 AM
02_BAL_05856_ch1_001_033.pdf	Cheryl Ball	Sep 29, 2020
Chapter 1 - 3e revision draft 1	me	8:19 AM

Shared with... > Writer/Desi... > REVISIONS

Figure 5.1 Sharing Files in Google Drive

Write/Design Toolkit

See "Organizing and Sharing Assets" (pp. 164–68), for more on version control and naming conventions.

Google Drive to manage our authoring process and then migrated to Dropbox so that we could provide better version control. For this edition, we decided to move back to Google Drive from the very beginning (see **Fig. 5.1**). Because we had difficulty keeping track of versions in our early editions, we created a standard naming convention for files shared only among the three authors. Once those final drafts were ready to pass along to our editor, they were placed in a second Google Drive folder so she didn't have to get bogged down with our day-to-day progress.

Sometimes we would all run into file-sharing problems, and miscommunications would lead to confusion. It happens even with the best of teams! So we start by providing strategies for keeping collaboration working and communication open among your teammates.

Strategies for Successful Collaboration

Just as every multimodal project is different, so is every collaborative situation. But there are some common strategies you can follow to make your group experience more successful and productive.

- If you have the option, limit the size of your team to between three and five members. Larger teams tend to have trouble coordinating schedules and coming to decisions (particularly when projects are designed as part of a class).

- If you get to choose your own team members, try to find others who will bring a diverse set of skills and perspectives to the process. Don't automatically choose friends or colleagues you already agree with. True collaboration means having divergent ideas and building consensus.

- Exchange contact information with the other team members, and commit to responding to them in a timely manner.

- Choose a preferred communication method where everyone on the team has access to all the information they need at any time. From experience, we can tell you that communicating via email, text message, and in-document comments can be difficult to keep track of, especially if all team members aren't included in every message. We recommend an online project management or communication tool—there are many freely available programs that support team-based work online (see **Fig. 5.2**).

- Create a group or team contract to spell out member expectations, such as roles, communication procedures, meeting guidelines, and problem-solving tactics.

- Be a good contributor—come to team meetings with all of your materials and with ideas about how to move the project forward. Just showing up and waiting around for someone to tell you what to do isn't really participation. And pull your own weight; nobody appreciates group members who don't complete their work.

- Be a good listener—collaborating requires that you listen to others' ideas and that you are open to other possibilities. You don't always have to agree, but try to give people a chance to make their case. It's especially important to encourage (and make space for) quieter members of your team to contribute.

- Remember that the most successful teams are often the ones whose members are flexible and are not so wedded to their

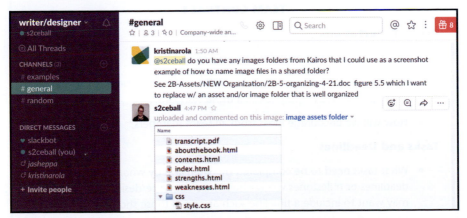

Figure 5.2 Discussing Book Revisions in Slack

The authors used Slack, a free communication tool that allows group chats and private messaging along with file uploads and linking to external services like Dropbox and Google Drive.

Cheryl Ball and Kristin Arola

ideas that they can't compromise. Being able to build off parts of one another's ideas can lead to some innovative and interesting possibilities.

- If your group faces *minor* conflict, try having a team meeting where members are asked to briefly share their perspectives on what's happening and their suggestions for resolving the issue. Be sure to listen for ways you can help improve group interaction or individual members' experiences to help move the project towards successful completion.

- If your group faces *serious* conflict, talk to your instructor or supervisor, who will likely have strategies for helping to mediate and move forward.

◉— Touchpoint: Write a Team Contract

One of the most helpful strategies for successful collaboration is to write a team contract. To begin, you and your fellow members should discuss group expectations, procedures, and project goals. Use the list of questions that follows to guide your initial planning conversations and to compose a team contract that spells out shared expectations. Depending on your group project's rhetorical situation, you may decide to add other areas of concern to the contract. This contract will help to set guidelines from the beginning and to hold your group accountable to one another. Be sure to write up, sign, and distribute a copy of this contract to every member of your team.

TEAM CONTRACT

Group Expectations

- What are our group goals for this project?

- What quality of work do we expect from each group member, and what strategies will we employ to fulfill these standards?

- How will we encourage ideas from all team members?

Tasks and Deadlines

- What tasks need to be completed by when and by whom? What kinds of deadlines or milestones will we build into our write/design process? You may want to include a timeline such as one of those shown at the end of Chapter 4 (p. 107).

Group Procedures

- What will be the dates, times, and locations of meetings?

- What is the preferred method of communication (communication app, email, a project-management system, texting, phone calls, face-to-face or videoconference meetings) for sharing information about meetings, updates, reminders, and problems?

- Where will assets and drafts be stored so that everyone who needs access has it?

Personal Accountability

- What strengths do individuals have that might make them more suited to one of the elements that needs to be produced more than others? How will you break up the workload in an equitable way?

- What is each team member's expected level of responsibility for attending meetings, responding to communication from other group members, and completing assigned tasks on time?

- How will the group handle a team member who does not comply with the contract? What are the consequences?

Collaborative Workflow Options

One of the biggest challenges of group work on multimodal projects is finding a way to meaningfully involve all group members and to divide work fairly and reasonably. The following examples demonstrate how three student groups managed this challenge.

- **Divide the Work by Project Sections.** In one of Cheryl's classes, a student group created a webtext about the visual rhetoric of movie posters in certain genres and across historical periods. The group decided that the project would have four main sections based on four movie genres and their representative posters: comedies, romantic comedies, action/thriller movies, and remakes (see **Fig. 5.3**). The four-person group divided the workload by movie genre so that each author was responsible for collecting assets and designing the Web page for a particular genre. The group members worked together to create the project's introduction and the works cited page. In **Figure 5.4**, the group's working file structure shows the breakdown of the project's workload.

> **Write/Design Toolkit**
>
> For more on arranging file structures, see "Organizing and Sharing Assets," (pp. 164–68).

- **Organize by Media Types and Expertise.** Another of Cheryl's student groups also created a webtext, this one about fashion and identity. The webtext included original fashion photos, video interviews of the authors discussing how fashion *shows*

Figure 5.3 Planned Home Page of the "Translating Movie Posters" Group Project

Courtesy Casey Kilroy, Erin Lentz, Jess Krist, and Brian Sorenson

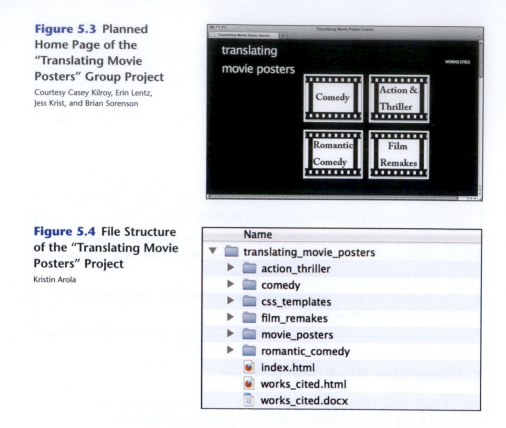

Figure 5.4 File Structure of the "Translating Movie Posters" Project

Kristin Arola

their identity, and scholarly sources that supported the visual components of the webtext. The three group members chose to break down their drafting process according to each student's expertise. Darien, an art and design major, was responsible for the website construction; Jenna, a publishing major, was responsible for the written text; and Bridget, a technical writing major, was responsible for the video editing. Because each member played to their strength, this small group was able to compose a large, ambitious project in a relatively short amount of time.

- **Organize by Compromise and Consensus.** The final student group, from Jenny's class, created an audio documentary on what it's like to be a search and rescue (SAR) team volunteer. The group was able to gather six hours of audio interviews, but then a critical issue emerged: How would the group decide which topics to develop and which to leave out due to time constraints? Each group member approached the project from a different perspective: one of them wanted to establish an "intellectually artful" feel, one wanted "to make an emotional appeal," and one wanted "to create a coherent story."

Each member listened to all six hours of audio and took notes on the themes and compelling stories they thought should be included. The group members were committed to compromise and worked together to decide on a few basic themes for the documentary. In the end, all the members felt that they had been listened to and that their priorities had been accommodated. They all reported that the experience was frustrating at times, but that their project was ultimately stronger because of the combination of ideas. Their final project was coherent and engaging and provided a strong sense of the joys and stresses of being a SAR volunteer.

◎— Touchpoint: **Planning with a Team**

Imagine that your residence hall floor or a campus club you belong to has decided to enter this year's EarthWeek competition at your school. EarthWeek is a series of events that encourage, celebrate, and advocate for sustainability, campus spirit, and diversity.

EarthWeek requires each team to submit the following four elements to be eligible to participate in the campus-wide competition:

1. A social media advertisement to inform the broader campus community about the EarthWeek event.

2. A one- to two-minute video advocating for the three pillars of EarthWeek: sustainability, diversity, and campus spirit.

3. An environmentally oriented game to teach visiting elementary students about sustainability and diversity at this year's festival.

4. An event of your own design that advocates and educates about at least one of the three pillars (you could arrange a special hike with a ranger at a nearby nature preserve, develop a composting program with campus restaurants and cafeterias, organize a beach cleanup, and lots more).

Given these requirements and this rhetorical situation, how would your team go about completing this work? Who will organize your first meeting to discuss initial ideas, and how will it be run to maximize input and participation? What other issues do you need to address to make sure your team's entry is competitive? To help you plan, consider the questions in the Touchpoint on writing a team contract (pp. 112–13).

Working Alone

You can create a strong multimodal project on your own, but there are a few useful things to remember.

- Working alone because you hate working in groups undercuts the potential of any project you might create. With others, you have more ideas, skills, and talents to work with.

- Since you won't have team members to bounce ideas off of, be sure to do a thorough job in preparing your pitch presentation and proposal (see Chapter 4). Doing so will allow you to get critical feedback from your instructor, classmates, or other stakeholders so that you can make adjustments as needed.

- Keep the size of your project manageable. Since you will be doing all the research, asset gathering, composing, and editing, you'll want to focus the scope of your ideas.

- Since you'll be solely responsible for the composing, seek out support for any technologies with which you're unfamiliar. We want to encourage you to try new genres, but if you run into trouble or have questions, consult with local resources, online tutorials, or friends. Just because you're working alone doesn't mean you can't get feedback or assistance from others.

◉— Touchpoint: Working Alone Isn't Really Working Alone

If it's not obvious from the tips above, we don't really believe it's possible to work absolutely by yourself on a project. There is always someone (or something) to provide feedback, advice, or information. In our own professional lives, we have found a mentoring map (see **Fig. 5.5**) to be surprisingly helpful to identify who might provide support—and a feedback loop—on a large project.

Think about the network of people who will support you and give you feedback on the work for which you're using this book. Then, fill out the map below. Keep it with you throughout your projects, adding people or groups as you discover them.

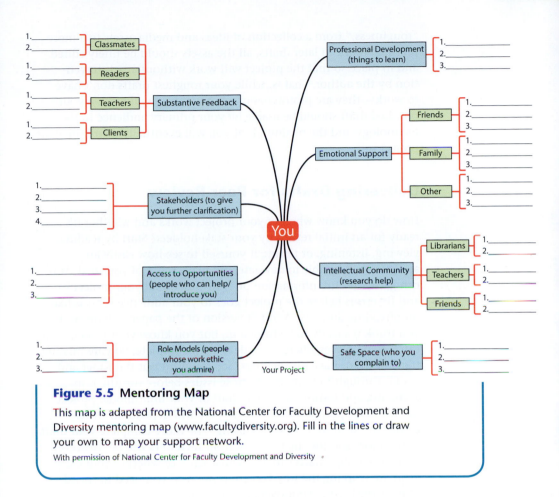

1._____
2._____ — Classmates

1._____
2._____ — Readers

1._____
2._____ — Teachers — Substantive Feedback

1._____
2._____ — Clients

Professional Development (things to learn)
1._____
2._____
3._____

Friends
1._____
2._____
3._____

Emotional Support — Family
1._____
2._____
3._____

Other
1._____
2._____
3._____

1._____
2._____
3._____
4._____ — Stakeholders (to give you further clarification)

You

1._____
2._____
3._____ — Access to Opportunities (people who can help/ introduce you)

Intellectual Community (research help)

Librarians
1._____
2._____

Teachers
1._____
2._____

Friends
1._____
2._____

1._____
2._____
3._____ — Role Models (people whose work ethic you admire)

Your Project

Safe Space (who you complain to)
1._____
2._____
3._____

Figure 5.5 Mentoring Map

This map is adapted from the National Center for Faculty Development and Diversity mentoring map (www.facultydiversity.org). Fill in the lines or draw your own to map your support network.

With permission of National Center for Faculty Development and Diversity

Putting Together a Complete Draft for Your Primary Audience

While team members and your support network function as one type of audience you work with when you're building your multimodal project, your primary audience for the project and its needs are always the most important. Because *how* the project progresses will also be dependent on what media and technologies you're working in, we have reserved discussion of those possibilities for Chapter 7, where you can pick and choose which you plan to make (i.e., analog or digital, dynamic or static, etc.). You might be drafting an outline, mock-up, storyboard, or prototype, depending on the media and technology choices that are appropriate to your audience. In any case, your project will move through various stages of "roughness," from a collection of ideas and media assets to a more polished draft. In later drafts, all the assets should be finely edited and in place so that the project will work without any intervention by the author. That is, while your roughest drafts don't have to work—they are prototypes of what you *hope* will work—your polished draft should be usable by your primary audience in the technology and the medium that you will eventually distribute your project in.

Delivering Drafts for Peer Review

How do you know whether your project works and whether it's ready for an initial review by your stakeholders? Start by reading, viewing, listening, or testing it yourself to see how easily an audience will be able to navigate and make sense of your text. You can gather useful information on how functional your project is and fix errors before the project goes to your audience. This is like proofreading an essay: A rough version of the paper is done, and you think it's ready to be turned in, but you know your teacher will catch some places where your ideas are incomplete, you are missing transitions, or have misspellings. So, you print out the paper and read it through to try to catch those issues before turning it in. Preparing and testing the rough draft of your multimodal project has the same purpose. How you prepare will depend on which media and technologies you're using. The more complete your draft is, the more specific the feedback from reviewers will be. However, even very rough drafts can give you a sense of whether your early ideas are working the way you envision, or if you need to spend time reconsidering your overall approach.

A useful review provides feedback on an author's in-progress work. When peers or other stakeholders provide feedback, they often intuitively understand the rhetorical situation and genre expectations of a text. Sometimes, however, reviewers don't know how to evaluate a project because they are not familiar with the particular situation or genre or because they are used to working on other kinds of projects. As a writer/designer, it is often helpful to provide some context for reviewers about the intended audience and purpose of your multimodal project so they can offer feedback that's relevant to your text's situation.

For instance, in the following example, a group of English department faculty members at West Virginia University, each with varying design expertise (from none to significant), discussed changes to a rough draft of an affirmation poster. The poster was designed in response to the rise in hate speech after the 2016 elections and a presidential executive order in early 2017 enacting a travel ban from Muslim majority countries. The English department wanted to hang the poster in the foyer to its campus building (see **Fig. 5.6**) as a way to encourage community building and unity through compassion and ethical communication. Because the English department faculty had expertise in language, the wording of the statement was completed quickly, through multiple rounds of feedback. But inserting the statement into a designed poster presented some feedback challenges. The poster, designed quickly by a local copy shop, was first distributed as an 8.5 × 11 inch color printout in a department meeting. That version was easy to pass around for comments, especially since the final poster was meant to be a large-scale 3 × 6 foot vertical poster, which would have been impossible to pass around to the thirty stakeholders present. Reviewers made various points

DEPARTMENT OF ENGLISH AFFIRMATION OF VALUES

We, the members of WVU's Department of English, believe that critical and creative reading and writing constitute acts of radical love. We ally ourselves with a multitude of departments, student bodies, and dedicated individuals across the country and the world who refuse to remain silent within a climate of hatred and violence: be it from sexism, racism, classism, ableism, nativism, anti-Semitism, misogyny, homophobia, transphobia, xenophobia, or Islamophobia. We are committed to building communities, not dividing them.

Colson Hall and our classrooms campus-wide are spaces where students, faculty, and staff may safely voice their concerns and where we may, together, foster futures more just. We aim to raise the status of those suppressed by the status quo; in assembly with human and nonhuman beings, we protest all types of environmental degradation, especially those prescribed at the expense of inhabitants' health.

Our research and syllabi affirm the core values of compassion, inclusivity, and care that a diverse humanities program holds for everyone. By telling stories of those who suffer under oppression in any form, past and present, we honor the ability of language and other means of communication—in each area of study we offer—to redress these wrongs, urge unity, and pursue peace. To those who seek shelter or wish to expand its scope, we welcome you; we thank you; we are with you.

West Virginia University

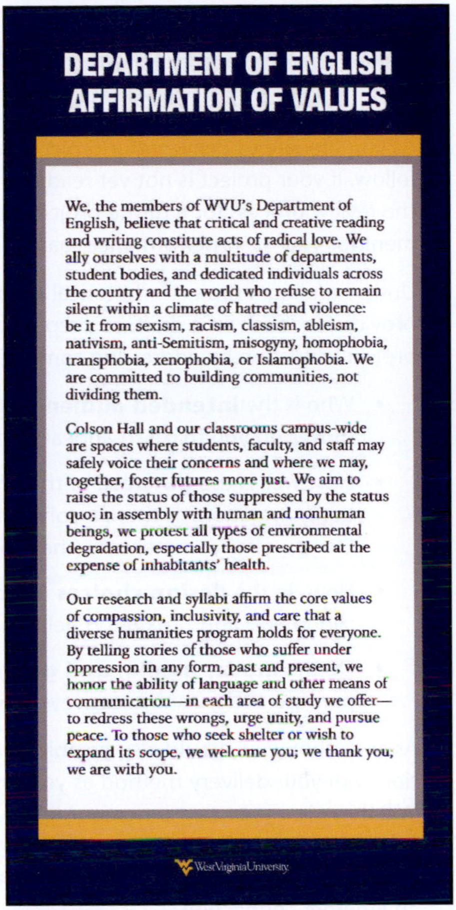

Figure 5.6 Final Draft of WVU Affirmation Poster
Courtesy West Virginia University Department of English

about the colors, typeface, and styles used in the poster. The more experienced design faculty noted that the design didn't quite meet the accepted WVU branding schema. After that initial review of the rough draft and several design revisions in Adobe InDesign by faculty members, a PDF was distributed on the department listserv and the final poster was approved and printed.

This is a brief example about how the formats of projects and stakeholders' knowledge of the project constraints might help (or sometimes hinder) getting feedback on your project. We discuss peer review more in the second half of this chapter, but there are other documents you can provide stakeholders to help them understand how to review your project. We detail these in the next section.

◎— Touchpoint: Preparing Audiences for Feedback with a Delivery Plan

As you prepare to deliver your project for review, consider the questions that follow. If your project is not yet ready for this stage, use this activity to plan for the review process for a future project, such as a research paper or advertisement for your next performance, game, or other event.

Understanding a project's rhetorical situation will prepare audiences to better provide feedback on a draft, so prepare a delivery plan that summarizes your project's situation by addressing some of the following questions:

- Who is the **intended audience** for this piece, and what rhetorical moves do you make to appeal to these readers/listeners/viewers/users?

- How well is the **purpose** of the project conveyed through its organization/navigation? Is there a coherent message for the audience to follow? Do you offer commentary (the "so what" of the argument or story)?

- How do the **design choices** (emphasis, contrast, organization, alignment, and proximity) help enact your purpose?

- Do the **mode, media, and genre** choices contribute to the overall purpose and meaning conveyed by the project?

As an author, you should also be able to accommodate your readers' interaction with your delivery method as you prepare for them to give you feedback. Will they view your text onscreen? If so, what kind of screen will they view it on—desktop, laptop, mobile, tablet? Where will they view it? In the library, in their home office, in a classroom, on a train? Will they view it over a wireless or an Ethernet connection?

- Where does the review take place?

- As the author, am I expected to be present during the review?

- If so, what are the presentation expectations? Is it formal or informal? What is the expected attire?

- If not, how will I provide reviewers with my draft?

- What technologies are available for them to review my project? For me to review their project?

- What's the timeline for reviewing? Will the review of each other's work take place at the same time? Is it limited to a classroom or meeting session? Do we each have a few days to review the work? What's the deadline?

- In what medium are the reviews to be conducted? If multimedia reviews (such as audio or screen recordings) are acceptable, is the author able to access reviews that are made in proprietary programs?

Peer Reviewing Multimodal Projects

While you may be eager to hear commentary about your own project, providing feedback to your colleagues can be equally valuable in terms of helping you think about different and successful approaches to multimodal projects. As a reviewer of someone else's work, you have three main tasks:

1. **Read/view/use the text** from the perspective of a particular audience member or rhetorical situation for which that text is intended (the summary of rhetorical situation and genre conventions in the Touchpoint Activity on page 120 is intended to assist readers with understanding this perspective).

2. **Evaluate** whether the text is successful at meeting the criteria and expectations required by that rhetorical situation.

3. **Provide constructive and specific feedback** to the author based on the text's effectiveness (or ineffectiveness).

Read/View/Use the Text

When reviewing a text, you should begin by familiarizing yourself with the rhetorical situation and genre expectations of the project. A summary or checklist like the one we recommended you create for the Touchpoint exercise, Preparing Audiences for Feedback with a Delivery Plan (p. 120), can be useful if you are unfamiliar with the genre, intended audience, or other elements of the rhetorical situation.

We had plenty of rough drafts for the first edition of this book—more than twenty, in fact—and another half-dozen for the second and third editions. Each time that we made revisions (using our editor and each other as our feedback loop), we used the Suggesting Mode in Google Docs (as shown in **Fig. 5.7**). Once our editor approved the revisions, she cleared them out (by accepting them) and continued revising other sections that still needed work.

You may need time to figure out how the text works and why it works the way it does, and to discover whether there are elements of what the author has designed that you like (or don't like). Try to give the whole text a read/view/use before writing out extensive comments that may not be relevant once you understand the project's big picture. Being an active reviewer—trying to figure out what the author's reasoning was for a particular design choice or rhetorical decision—will aid you in providing constructive feedback. In other words, don't just assume an author did it wrong. As you read, take notes on how and why you respond to the piece.

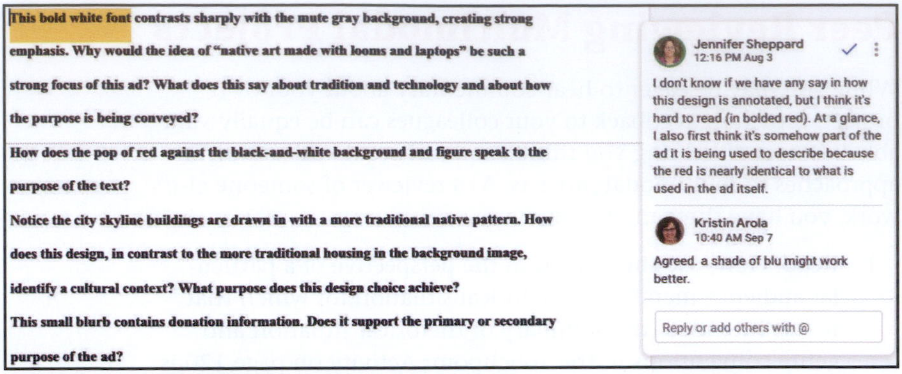

This bold white font contrasts sharply with the mute gray background, creating strong emphasis. Why would the idea of "native art made with looms and laptops" be such a strong focus of this ad? What does this say about tradition and technology and about how the purpose is being conveyed?

How does the pop of red against the black-and-white background and figure speak to the purpose of the text?

Notice the city skyline buildings are drawn in with a more traditional native pattern. How does this design, in contrast to the more traditional housing in the background image, identify a cultural context? What purpose does this design choice achieve?

This small blurb contains donation information. Does it support the primary or secondary purpose of the ad?

Jennifer Sheppard 12:16 PM Aug 3

I don't know if we have any say in how this design is annotated, but I think it's hard to read (in bolded red). At a glance, I also first think it's somehow part of the ad it is being used to describe because the red is nearly identical to what is used in the ad itself.

Kristin Arola 10:40 AM Sep 7

Agreed. a shade of blu might work better.

Reply or add others with @

Figure 5.7 A Rough Draft with Feedback in Google Docs
Jennifer Sheppard

This is where the summary of the rhetorical situation created by the author can serve as a touchstone for evaluating the project.

Evaluate the Text

Based on your reading of the project, it's your job as a reviewer to evaluate how effectively the designer hits the rhetorical mark. As a reader, do you feel that the project meets your needs and expectations? Does it miss anywhere? For each question or comment that you pose to the writer/designer, you should be able to include discussion of *why* and *how* in your review.

Here are some suggested questions to ask yourself as you evaluate the text:

- Does the project match the expected **rhetorical situation** and **genre conventions** to meet the audience's needs? If not, does it break those conventions in productive ways that serve the audience?

- How do the **mode**, **media**, and **genre** choices contribute to the overall purpose and meaning conveyed by the project? Are there any you would add or delete, and if so, why?

- Is the **design** of this project appropriate to its **purpose**? If some design choices seemed inappropriate in relation to the rhetorical situation, what suggestions would you make for revising?

- How credible do you find the **assets** and **sources** used for the project's argument? Were there any sources you found problematic? If so, which ones and why, and what would you suggest be used in their place? Were there sources missing that you'd suggest for the project?

Write/Design Toolkit

See "Collecting Assets" (p. 146) and "Working with Multimodal Sources" (p. 148) for more information on collecting and working with assets.

Provide Constructive and Specific Feedback

In preparing your review from your reading notes, you should identify the main strengths and weaknesses of the project, summarizing your thoughts about how well the piece addresses the rhetorical situation. Discuss how the piece meets (or doesn't meet) the project criteria, and provide specific and constructive feedback, including revision suggestions whenever possible. In many cases, reviews of rough drafts are written up and provided to the authors so that they can refer to the review comments throughout the revision process. Those review comments provide overarching commentary on the status of the piece, summarizing what suggestions you have for further strengthening this author's approach or for better attending to the target audience. They can also offer specific revision suggestions.

Here are some tips for writing a useful review:

- Use the beginning of the review to summarize the project's purpose back to the author, which helps the author see whether you understood the piece in the way that they intended or in a different way.

- Be generous in your reading, and be helpful and productive in explaining what's not working in the piece and how you think the author should revise the project. Use a tone that will help the author take in your advice rather than just be frustrated or offended by it. Help the author recognize what is working so that they can build on those positive aspects in revising.

- The review should usually address revision suggestions in a hierarchical way, moving from the biggest issues to the smallest issues. Small issues are sometimes left out of the review if big picture issues overwhelm the project. For example, it may not be important that a project has some grammatical errors if it's not hitting the mark as far as its overall purpose.

- Alternately, a review might be structured as a reader response—that is, it might follow the reader's chronological progression through the text. But summaries at the beginning and end of the review are still helpful in contextualizing the reviewer's minute-by-minute commentary.

- Always explain why and how a project is or isn't working well, and make sure that your revision suggestions are clear, even if your revision ideas are more like suggestions than must-dos.

◉— Touchpoint: Giving Feedback on a Rough Draft

Ask your classmates, instructor, or other stakeholder to review your multimodal project, and offer your services as a reviewer in turn. Using the questions outlined in the Peer Reviewing Multimodal Projects section above, write a peer-review letter to another author that follows the tips and steps for giving constructive feedback: (1) read the text, (2) evaluate the text, and (3) provide constructive feedback on the text.

You might also consider creating more specific peer-review questions for the genre of text you are reviewing. For instance, students in one of Jenny's classes used the following questions to peer review a genre-analysis infographic. How can you rephrase some of these to get at the reading, evaluation, and constructive feedback of your own peer-review letter?

- Who is the **audience**, and how can you tell? Is there any information that needs to be added or taken away to make it more useful to target readers?

- What is the **purpose** of this project? That is, what do you take away as a reader and how well does this seem to match up with the intentions of the writer/designer?

- Has the designer kept it simple? Is there too much or too little information? If so, what specific suggestions do you have?

- What **design principles** are used, and in what ways are they relevant to **emphasize** significant content (**contrast**), maintain visual unity (**repetition**), **organize** information, and group related content (**alignment**, **proximity**, **framing**)? What suggestions do you have for improvement?

- Name one thing that the **designer does particularly well** in this draft.

- What other suggestions or ideas do you have for improving the message of the text?

CASE STUDY

Revising an Advertisement Design with Stakeholder Feedback

As part of her job, Cheryl helps a nonprofit organization called the Council of Editors of Learned Journals (CELJ). This organization is composed of hundreds of scholarly journal editors who discuss editorial issues related to their individual journals in a private, online forum where they can seek advice and information from other editors in a confidential manner. One of the member benefits for journal editors is a discounted advertisement in an internationally renowned glossy magazine called the *Times Literary Supplement* (*TLS*), and the CELJ gets a free advertisement each year in the *TLS* because of all the additional ad revenue it brings to the *TLS* through its members. (All of this is **context** for the *what*, which comes next.) The *TLS* sent Cheryl the following email to forward to members, reminding them to place their ads, including CELJ's own ad.

Dear CELJ Member, ●————————————— Stakeholder

The *Times Literary Supplement* is the world's oldest and most reputable literary journal. It is published every Friday, and reviews thousands of — Context books every year. It has a growing circulation—currently around 28,000
Audience
per week—and its readers are mature, affluent, and well educated.
Client
The October 28th issue of the *TLS* will offer members of the CELJ the — Purpose opportunity to advertise their journals at half the regular price.

This issue will carry three or four pages of reviews of journals, and — **Additional context about visual layout, organization** another 3 or 4 pages of advertising.
Genre conventions
Advertising in this issue starts at £57.50 for the minimum 5 cm x 6.3 cm box, and there is a huge range of sizes available.

If you have any questions, or if you would like to book some space in this
Stakeholder
issue, please contact email-redacted@tlk.uk. The deadline for this issue is fast
Context (due date)
approaching—space needs to be confirmed before October 14th.

Cheryl knew the **audience** would be educated and well-read readers of the *Times Literary Supplement,* which is a premier print-based literary and cultural magazine that has been around for over 100 years. But the CELJ ad didn't need to target just *any* reader of the *TLS*; it needed to target editors of literary and scholarly journals who read the *TLS*. Cheryl had to design the ad to effectively target readers of *TLS* who were also editors, to persuade them to join CELJ.

Cheryl (as an intermediate stakeholder/client) asked Lydia, a project team member, to design a rough draft of the ad that Cheryl could modify or approve before sending it to the magazine for publication. This email helped Lydia understand the rhetorical situation for designing the ad. Cheryl instructed Lydia to use the following elements in her draft of the ad: the

Write/Design Toolkit

See "Collecting Assets" (p. 146) for tips on how to gather design assets, like Lydia did for her advertisement.

CELJ logo, a list of the organization's member benefits, a link to its website, and the sponsoring institution (their university library). Lydia was able to easily gather all those assets from other projects she had worked on with Cheryl to design a draft of the ad well before the deadline.

But not all of the context Lydia needed to design the ad was present in the initial email that the *TLS* sent out. For instance, she had to ask several questions of the contact person at the magazine:

1. What size/dimensions could CELJ use?

2. Where would the final advertisement appear—online or in print? (The delivery medium would impact color choices and the image resolution.)

3. If it would appear in print, what kind of paper would the magazine use? (Printing on matte, glossy, or newsprint paper requires different design techniques that affect how the ink soaks into the paper.)

4. If in print, would the ad appear in black-and-white or in color (and if the latter, how many colors would she be allowed—since color printing can often come in variants of one, two-, three-, or four-color combinations)?

5. Finally, in what technical format would they prefer delivery of the ad file(s)? (JPEG, PNG, etc.)

In this case, the ad would appear only in the printed version of the magazine, alongside other ads for journals. The magazine gave advertisers two options for sending: either a designed ad in the form of a 10-cm high × 13-cm wide PDF, or text and logos so the magazine could design the ad. Cheryl and Lydia decided to send a designed ad so they would have more control over the CELJ branding. The magazine did not give any color restrictions, but Cheryl and Lydia chose to design the ad minimalistically, with the single, blue color that matches the CELJ logo and website branding. They also knew that since the ad would appear alongside several other journal advertisements on a single page, they wanted the CELJ ad to stand out from the crowd and so used white space to accomplish that goal.

Lydia was nervous. She didn't think she was a good visual designer, so the task of designing an ad was daunting. But she stepped up to the challenge and designed several mock-ups and drafts, delivering them to Cheryl for initial feedback as both a Portable Document Format (PDF) and a Photoshop Data file (.psd) (see **Fig. 5.8**). Lydia knew that Cheryl had access to Adobe Photoshop, an image manipulation program installed on her computer, so it was OK to send her a copy of the editable .psd file. But if Cheryl hadn't

Council of Editors of Learned Journals

MEMBER BENEFITS   JOIN TODAY

- Guaranteed exhibit space at MLA   For more information,
- Advertising discount at Times Literary   visit celj.org.
  Supplement
- Access to a members-only editorial discussion
  forum
- Outreach opportunities with editors
  nationwide

Figure 5.8 Initial Draft of the Ad in Photoshop

Courtesy of the Council of Editors of Learned Journals

had Photoshop, she would not have been able to open or view the .psd file. (That's why it's important to remember to send your reviewers the project and file types they can open and read, just like you would in the final version of the text.)

Lydia worked diligently to manipulate Photoshop to produce an initial draft in **Figure** 5.8. Later that same day, when she was on a computer without Photoshop, she continued to create mock-ups of her ideas using PowerPoint (**Fig. 5.9**). It's typical for designers to create three to four mock-ups or roughly designed drafts for the client to choose from. (In this case, Cheryl would

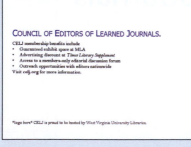

Mock-Up #1 Lydia played with variations of alignments and white space.

Mock-Up #2 Lydia played with minimal
alignment and white space even more.

Figure 5.9 PowerPoint Mock-ups.

Courtesy of the Council of Editors of Learned Journals

choose for CELJ.) Lydia's primary concern at this point was to make sure the layout of the ad met the constraints given by the magazine: the size and dimension requirements.

Cheryl liked the general direction Lydia was heading with the Photoshop draft. She provided feedback for Lydia to revise the ad so it made better use of the **design concepts** Lydia had started with, including her attention to proximity, alignment, color, organization, and emphasis. Cheryl could have written up the feedback for Lydia but decided to meet with her instead to show her some additional design resources she could draw on to feel more comfortable designing such ads in the future.

Cheryl's reading notes from Lydia's first draft included the notes annotated in **Figure 5.10**, as well as some more general thoughts, perspectives, and reactions:

- The information Lydia included in the ad was appropriate, and the way it was grouped was effective. It's easy to tell what the main information is—the CELJ header, Member Benefits, and Join Today are emphasized through size, color, and all caps.

The color of the CELJ "header" matches the logo for visual repetition and cohesion. But the thinness of the CELJ header font counteracts its level of emphasis, and there was a lot of space between the top and second rows of that header.

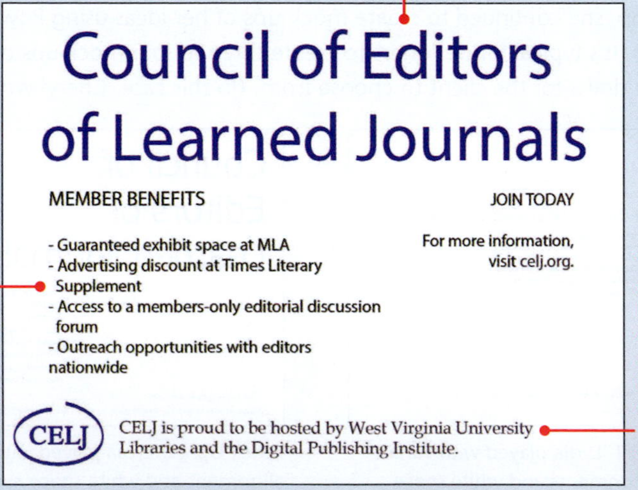

The dashes used as bullet points and the lack of hanging indents on the list made this rough draft seem rougher than it needed to be. The *TLS* would expect a little more polish.

The footer information, with the logo, should be centered to retain alignment with the header and body copy, as well as to avoid trapped white space in the lower right corner.

Council of Editors of Learned Journals

MEMBER BENEFITS   JOIN TODAY

- Guaranteed exhibit space at MLA   For more information,
- Advertising discount at Times Literary   visit celj.org.
  Supplement
- Access to a members-only editorial discussion
  forum
- Outreach opportunities with editors
  nationwide

 CELJ is proud to be hosted by West Virginia University
Libraries and the Digital Publishing Institute.

Figure 5.10 Cheryl's Feedback on the Draft

Courtesy of the Council of Editors of Learned Journals; (Annotations) Courtesy of Cheryl Ball

- The design was fuzzy for some reason (this could be OK for a rough draft, but not a final draft).

- The varying fonts—*serif* in the "footer" copy versus *sans serif* in the "body" copy—were easy to read on their own, but together they conflicted with each other in style and color.

- The left and right alignments were working well, with a two-column layout.

After revising based on Cheryl's feedback, Lydia and Cheryl produced the version shown in **Figure 5.11**. In this version, they changed the fonts so that the CELJ header font more closely matched the font used in the logo and made the header the central feature of the ad, with smaller spacing between each line, which gives the words better **proximity** to show their grouping as a single **linguistic** element in the ad. Lydia and Cheryl also removed the bullet points in the benefits listing so that its sentence-like structure would work with the footer copy to **frame** the CELJ header as the ad's focal point. In addition, the footer was edited so it would all fit on one line, while still retaining its original meaning. The shorter line also added white space above the footer, further emphasizing the CELJ header. Finally, since the ad would appear amidst several pages with nothing but advertisements for other journals and on a white, printed background, they added one final touch: a thin, blue stroke, or outline, for **emphasis** and **contrast**.

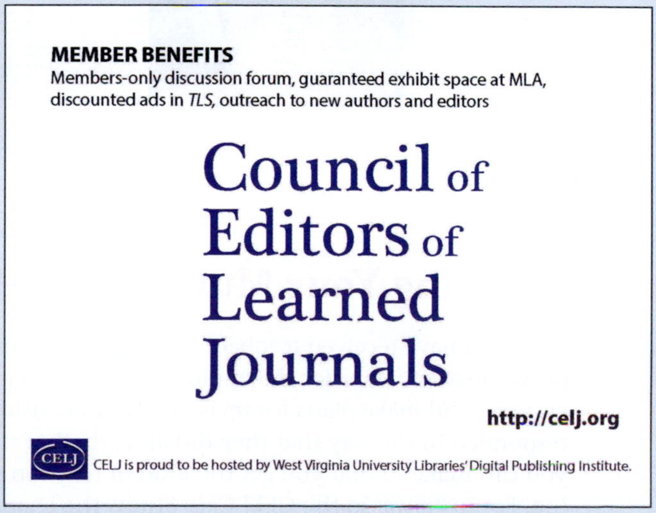

Figure 5.11
The Final Version of the CELJ Ad

Courtesy of the Council of Editors of Learned Journals

MEMBER BENEFITS
Members-only discussion forum, guaranteed exhibit space at MLA, discounted ads in *TLS*, outreach to new authors and editors

Council of Editors of Learned Journals

http://celj.org

 CELJ is proud to be hosted by West Virginia University Libraries' Digital Publishing Institute.

Finally, the *TLS* requested a PDF of the ad output from Photoshop, which Cheryl and Lydia did by sending them a link to a file-sharing location because—due to the print nature of the ad, which requires higher resolutions and larger file sizes than digitally distributed ads—the file was too large to send as an email attachment. It appeared several months later in the printed magazine alongside other ads (see **Fig. 5.12**).

Figure 5.12 The Final Version of the CELJ Ad in the Printed *TLS* (middle, left)

Courtesy Karen Lunsford

Revising Your Multimodal Project

After you have received feedback on your rough draft from your peers, instructor, and/or stakeholders, it's time to evaluate the suggestions and make plans for revision. Try to consider *why* reviewers responded in the way that they did and whether there are changes you can make so that you get the kind of reaction you were intending. For instance, in the CELJ Case Study, the change of spacing, proximity, emphasis, and other design choices during revision helped the advertisement more clearly stand out for readers amid a sea of other ads.

Creating a Revision Plan

After reviewing all feedback, you should assess which revisions are important given your project goals. Note that sometimes reviewers have bad days, or they don't understand your rhetorical situation (because they aren't the intended audience), or multiple reviewers may offer conflicting advice. But don't let yourself be fooled into thinking that you are always right and that your project doesn't need any revisions. If a majority of your reviewers indicated that your image choices are inappropriate for your project's audience or purpose, or that your script's tone is condescending, they are probably right. In addition, if a majority of your reviewers didn't mention a particular problem, but one reviewer made a *really good argument* for revising and backed it up with evidence from your text and your rhetorical situation summary, it's likely that the suggestion is a good one, and you'll need to consider addressing it as well.

Paying close attention to the feedback you've received, create a revision plan for your project. Here are some questions to help you determine which revisions you need to make:

- What were the strengths of my draft that I should keep?

- What design choices were problematic, and how can I revise these?

- What rhetorical choices seemed out of place in my draft, and how can I better attend to my audience, purpose, context, and genre?

- What multimodal elements can I add or revise to strengthen the rhetorical effect and credibility of my project?

- What are the most important changes I need to consider as I revise?

- Given the time and technology constraints of this project, what can I reasonably revise before the next due date? What else would need revision that I don't have time to complete but *should* complete, given enough time and resources?

That last question in the list is an important one. Most projects have a set deadline, whether it's a class project, a client's product-reveal date, or an event on the calendar. You and your reviewers may agree during the feedback loop and discussion of the revision plan that your original scope of work outlined in a proposal or assignment is too large to complete by the deadline but that a modified version of the project would be suitable for now. As long as you both agree to the modifications, it is fine to scale back on the scope of your project. In fact, scaling back may even strengthen your project.

Finalizing Your Project

After you've agreed to a revision plan, revise your rough draft into your final project. Your task is to make recommended changes and put the finishing touches on your project so that it accomplishes all your rhetorical goals. You will want to ensure that

- all of the multimodal elements you've included are purposeful;
- all of the multimodal elements support the credibility of your project;
- your audience can understand and navigate, view, or read your text as you intend.

Test your project by using it in a venue as close to its final publication or presentation location as possible. For instance, if you're making a video for a nonprofit organization that is meant to be shared through social media, try uploading the video to the location you will share it from—but only if you can mark the video as private so that it won't be released to the public before it's ready. Then share the private URL with a few key stakeholders or peers to see whether they think the revisions you've done match your rhetorical intentions. They may not have seen the original draft, so you might ask them key questions targeted to the purpose of the revisions after they've viewed it. That way, you won't end up with unnecessary revisions that this new audience prefers but that are not in the wishes of your teacher or other stakeholder. Tweak the project based on their feedback, revising as necessary until you're satisfied that the text does its rhetorical work or until you're out of time.

◉— **Touchpoint: Revising Your Project**

Using the suggested questions in the Creating a Revision Plan section (pp. 131–32), design a revision plan for your project that you can use as a task list for yourself or as a part of the documentation you hand over to stakeholders (discussed in the next section, "Creating Documentation for Your Stakeholders") if you don't have time to complete the revisions yourself. There are dozens of to-do apps online. Find one that suits your team's needs and use it to create a sharable revision plan with assigned tasks. Alternatively, create a shared list in Google Drive or a content management system that team members and stakeholders, such as your instructor, can view and use.

A Checklist for Final Drafts

Use the following list as a starting point of things to check for as you prepare the polished draft of your project for audience feedback.

- ❏ All written content has been finalized, edited, and proofread.

- ❏ All visual and aural elements (photos, illustrations, logos, videos, audio clips) have been edited in the appropriate software to their exact lengths or sizes and converted to the correct formats and resolutions, and they have been placed in their exact locations within the project.

- ❏ Fonts, text sizes, and color schemes have been implemented consistently throughout the document.

- ❏ Styles (when appropriate) have been used, and style guides have been followed.

- ❏ Animations (title screens, visual transitions, object movement) have been edited, synced for appropriate duration on screen, and placed in their final locations in the project.

- ❏ Color photocopies of all visual elements have been printed at the quality needed.

- ❏ Soundtracks or other whole-project media elements have been edited for appropriate volume, added to the timeline, and synced to the individual scenes or navigation.

- ❏ Navigation or movement within the project (prezi path, slide-show autoplay, Web menu, performance blocking) has been created and finalized.

- ❏ Nothing is broken (images are in place, links work, videos don't stall, programs don't crash).

- ❏ The analog project is available in its final medium (printed poster, folded brochure) or the digital project has been exported from its editing program (Word, InDesign, Canva Photoshop iMovie, Audacity, Dreamweaver, KompoZer) into the final output format (converted to a PDF, MP4 or MP3 file; moved onto a Web server).

You might consult your instructor, peers, other stakeholders, and/or intended audience at any stage, but once you have a completed draft (following the guidelines above), you should definitely seek feedback, even though it may not be totally ready for public release.

Creating Documentation for Your Stakeholders

While your primary audience takes priority in your design process, your prioritizations in a project are almost always built on other stakeholder's expectations, such as grading criteria developed by a teacher, project specs provided by a client, the budget available from a funding agency, and so on. When you work with stakeholders, keep their needs and expectations in mind throughout and even after the design process, since many times you might need to turn the project over to them upon its completion—either so they can archive it, continue running it, or update it in the future, as needed.

Clients will often continue working on projects after you've finished designing them, especially if you're volunteering, getting paid with one-time grant funds, or participating in a service-learning class. Projects such as newsletters, training materials, blogs, and other serialized or continually updated texts often have a series of people working on them, which increases the likelihood that the texts will remain active and useful. **Documentation** explains how a project was created, how to use it, or how to update it in the future. Writing documentation can also help project teams collaborate while they are drafting and serve as accessibility documentation for primary or secondary readers with different abilities who may not be able to read all of the media and modes you plan to use.

There are many kinds of documentation, such as white papers, reference manuals, online help files, and user guides. We explain two types of documentation methods: wikis and comments. Depending on your project, you may need one or both of those methods, or you may use some other method or combination of methods to convey your processes to your client. No matter which documentation method you choose, the rhetorical considerations we've used throughout this book will be effective when considering medium, genre, or technology.

Collaborative Wiki

In **Figure 5.13**, you can see some of the documentation developed by a team of student writer/designers who created an online literary arts magazine called *Din*. The students who created *Din* wanted future classes of students to be able to put out new editions of the magazine. They decided to use a wiki for their documentation, which allows all registered users to add to and edit the text. This wiki contains specifics about what design elements (in relation to

Figure 5.13 **Project Documentation in a Wiki**

The project documentation for *Din* illustrates and discusses logo and visual design choices.

Courtesy Jen Almjeld

rhetorical choices) the design group used to distribute iterations of the magazine to social media; it also hosts an archive of promotional materials and logo designs. In the future, the documentation wiki could easily be changed as needed. To see how editors comment on their changes to wikis, go to Wikipedia, search for a term related to your project, and click that entry's "View history" tab to see what kind of changes have happened recently.

In-Line Comments

A website designer will often embed comments into the HTML code to help future designers understand the designer's thought process when creating the site (**Fig. 5.14**). Comments do not show up on the actual Web page but are viewable in a browser's source code and in Web-editing programs like Dreamweaver or KompoZer. If you are working on a project that is not Web-based, you could use the marginal comments and balloons in word-processing programs to achieve a similar purpose.

To see this source code documentation at work, go to a website that you use often and view its code. (The code is sometimes found under View > Source, or you can search for instructions for finding the source code if it's not readily apparent.) How did the designers of the site use HTML commenting? If they didn't use commenting, are there places where it would have been useful?

Figure 5.14 Source Code Comments Can Provide Help for Future Users

Jeff Kuure

◉— Touchpoint: Creating a Style Guide

Documentation comes in many forms, including style guides. A style guide is a set of agreed-upon standards that a group uses to write, design, and edit documents. For example, look at the branding page for West Virginia University (http://brand.wvu.edu/). Brands include style guides (**Fig. 5.15**), and this website outlines why the "Mountaineers Go First!" rallying cry isn't

Figure 5.15 A Snapshot of the WVU Brand Center's Style Guide for Multiple Genres, Modes, and Text Usages

West Virginia University

just for football games: "Having the courage to go first doesn't mean going impulsively without a plan. Going first is about making bold, but informed decisions. As writers, designers, photographers, web developers and overall brand ambassadors, all of us are called upon to go forth and help shape our brand. This guide will direct you — ensuring that we communicate consistently and powerfully."

Now, create your own style guide for your multimodal project using the guidelines here. Remember that a style guide helps to create a consistent, unified project by making sure that all elements are used in the same way in all parts of your project. (You may need to refer to the appropriate sections in Part Two of this book to answer some of these questions. It's OK to skip ahead and read those now, then return to this Touchpoint later.)

1. Discuss with your project team the best way to organize, share, and design your assets, based on the best practices you have found through your research and drafting.

2. Include a listing of all visual choices, if relevant, that will be used throughout your project. This may include elements such as typefaces, text sizes, colors, and image sizes. It might also include guidelines for how media assets, such as video and audio clips, are embedded in a project.

3. Include plans for naming, storing, and sharing assets and style instructions.

4. Include a brief description of why your group has chosen to follow this particular style, based on the technologies you plan to use and the kinds of assets you found.

5. Decide where you will maintain your project style guide and how team members and stakeholders will have access to refer to and update it, as needed.

Reporting and Reflecting on Your Project

You may be asked to provide different kinds of **reports** throughout the multimodal composition process for your instructor or stakeholders. Status reports are usually written summaries of key progress made or milestones reached on the project, although they might occasionally be delivered as oral presentations. In contrast, end-of-project reporting can take the form of many different genres, including presentations, written reports, white papers, technical papers, scholarly articles, news features, and less formal genres such as blog posts, reflections, and exit interviews. In any of these genres, you have an opportunity to demonstrate to your audience the value of what you've done and (in some cases) the reasoning that got you to that point. If you are required to report on your multimodal project, keep in mind that your task is to be persuasive, not just descriptive. Help your audience understand each of the major design and rhetorical choices you've made and how those choices were appropriate to that particular rhetorical situation. **Reflecting** on your research and design processes as well as on your final project also allows you to see just how much you've learned and how you might approach your next project differently to make it even stronger and more efficient.

Sometimes reports indicate when an unforeseen problem has occurred and give the author a chance to explain the obstacle and provide a solution for overcoming it, which is especially useful in status reports or revision plans. Here's a typical example of a funding agency's reporting guidelines (from the Andrew W. Mellon Foundation) that requires a description of activities during the project:

- a summary of the project and purpose of the grant
- progress made towards the expected outcomes of the grant [project] and any other significant accomplishments
- any setbacks or challenges
- significant board, management, or staff changes
- plans and goals for the upcoming reporting period or, in the case of the final report, of the period subsequent to the grant

Discussing setbacks can be tricky. However, it's important for your teacher or other stakeholders to understand what work has been completed, what challenges have been encountered, what remains to be done, and how that work will be accomplished.

So, how do you focus on the lessons you learned in a report?

Phillip, a student in one of Jenny's classes, designed the "Scholarship Remixed" flyer in **Figure 5.16** and was required to write a final report for that project. In the excerpt that follows, you can see how Phillip researched the flyer genre, brainstormed by sketching initial ideas, and worked through the criteria for the assignment to consider the rhetorical situation. His report discusses his design and rhetorical choices, and it reflects on his composing process to analyze what worked well and how he might improve both the flyer and his design process in the future.

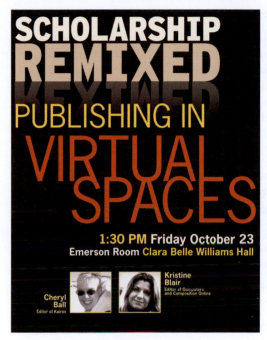

Figure 5.16 A Flyer Advertising a Speaking Event

Courtesy of Phillip Johnson

Preproduction Process

I started out thinking about what ideas or images the words might evoke. I gravitated towards the "Scholarship Remixed: Publishing in Virtual Spaces" title because the ideas of remixing and spaces open up lots of possibilities.

I surfed my favorite design sites to look at typefaces and color schemes. I also sketched some drawings to work out the density and hierarchy of the information and to work through a few layout ideas. I decided fairly early on this would be a typographic layout and that I wanted it to be bold in order to stand out from the clutter of a bulletin board.

Rhetorical Choices

I suppose the decision to focus on producing a typographic layout is the main rhetorical choice I made. Given that the audience for this presentation is mainly English students, it seemed appropriate to focus on the words and try to find ways to make them interesting without losing readability or clarity. For me, the purpose of a flyer like this is to convince people to show up by focusing on the *what*, along with the *where* and *when*. Towards that end, I made sure that the time and place info is not hidden or ambiguous.

Design Principles

Repetition is present in the design and is most apparent in the treatment of the photos and the accompanying text, even though the elements are not exact repeats. Colors also repeat to help unify and balance the design. Alignment is working with the various type elements on a number of levels. Proximity is most obvious in the relationship of the photos to each other and to their accompanying text.

Type

As this was always intended to be a typographic design, I spent a lot of time picking out the typefaces. I used Interstate for the bolder typeface at the top of the design, along with a few variants of News Gothic for everything else. I like the contrast between the two typefaces.

Here are some questions you should consider when reporting on your multimodal project to your stakeholders or clients:

- What were the primary ideas and intentions that guided your project?
- What were the key **rhetorical choices** you made?
- What was your **purpose** in creating this project?
- Who was your intended **audience**, and what did you do to attend to their needs or interests?
- What **context** did you design this project to be used in, and why?
- How did you select the **genre** that you used for your project?
- What were the key **design choices** you made? How did you make use of emphasis, contrast, organization, alignment, and proximity?
- What shaped your decisions about the **arrangement** of elements in your project, whether on paper, on screen, or in video or audio?
- What were your key **modal choices**? Which modes did you use, and why?
- What shaped your **dissemination choices** for how and where you would share your project with your audience?
- What were your most significant **project challenges and successes** as you planned, researched, drafted, and revised your multimodal project?
- What would you do differently if you started over? What lessons did you learn that can be applied to future projects?

write/design! assignment

Reporting on Your Project

Analyze the situation to determine what kind of project report you should create to fulfill your assignment or stakeholder's needs. Use the questions in the previous section (or others you and your instructor, stakeholder, or supervisor create) to produce a status report or final report on your multimodal project for your stakeholders.

You might also use other documentation you've created for your project along the way, including the proposal, rough draft summary, style guide, delivery plan, and revision plan. Depending on your client's needs, your final report might include all of the major texts you've produced as part of this project, but it might also need to be short and to the point, pulling together the most relevant information about the project and process for the stakeholders. If you're writing the final report, a key issue to address is where the project itself resides or how it will be delivered—your delivery plan.

> **Write/Design Toolkit**
>
> To help build out your delivery plan, refer to "Preparing for the Multimodal Afterlife" (pp. 198–200).

Here are some additional points to cover in your final report:

- **Overview:** What are the major rhetorical goals of your project? How were they met?
- **Audience:** Who are the target readers/users/viewers of the project, and what design choices have you made to accommodate them?
- **Design:** What ideas guided your organization of this project? If it's a print text, presentation, or webtext, what key elements were included, where were they placed, and why? If it's a video, audio, or animation project, what guidelines did you follow for how elements were ordered, what transitions were used, and/or how editing decisions were made?
- **Media:** What stylistic considerations did you make for images, audio, or video used in the project, and why?

If this is a status report, you should also include a section that describes what's going well or wrong, as well as any additional challenges the project is facing. All of these documents together will help you form a more sustainable documentation guide for your audience, clients, instructor, or stakeholders. Once you've finished the final report and the project, make plans to turn these materials over to the appropriate stakeholder—your instructor or a different audience. Unless you and your instructor or stakeholder have arranged for further upkeep on the project after you've turned it in, you're done. Congratulations!

write/design! option: Reflecting on Your Project

Perhaps you didn't work for a stakeholder other than your instructor. Or, perhaps in addition to the final reporting, your instructor or supervisor wants you to reflect on your learning throughout the design process—this is a great way to show your personal growth as a writer/designer. You can still refer back to and include any previous texts you created for your project, such as a proposal, style guide, or delivery plan. In fact, you may be required to if you're creating a portfolio for your project or course.

In addition, you might be asked to reflect on how the project you created meets the learning goals of the rhetorical situation or course. You might be asked to document why the design, media, and modal choices were important ones to reach your audience and what you learned by doing so. This document should be as long as your instructor requires, so make sure you continue to perform those genre and rhetorical analysis skills even on reflection documents. Now that you've been through the whole multimodal composition process, the workflows you used in this book will be helpful regardless of genre and modality. Good luck!

PART TWO

The Write/Design Toolkit

Working with Multimodal Assets and Sources

6

You probably know the term **sources** already, but what are **assets**? *Sources* are texts, such as books, articles, websites, and so on, that you can use to gather information about a topic or genre. Assets are pieces of content you'll actually use in your project. An *asset* might be a quotation, an image, a video clip, or a screenshot. For instance, let's say that for your project you need a twenty-second clip from a two-minute YouTube video. The source is the two-minute video (akin to a book or an article you pull from a shelf or the Web). The twenty-second clip from the video is your asset. You'll gather assets from your sources (see Fig. 6.1)—and, depending on your project, you might create your own assets (for example, by filming an interview with a friend).

Websites and other digital media are updated frequently, so it's important that you save a copy of any asset you think you may want to use when you first find it. Things on the Web disappear.

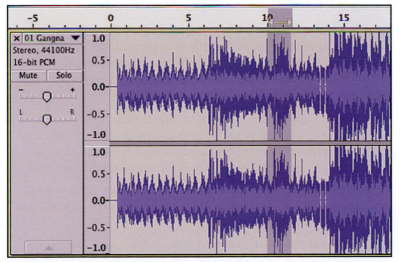

Figure 6.1 A Source and an Asset

In this waveform illustration of an audio clip, the entire song is the **source**, while the grayed-out selection between the ten-second mark and the eleven-and-a-half-second mark is the **asset** that will be used in the project.

For example, Jenny was giving a presentation about online adoption profiles and had planned to show a couple's website while she talked. She did not take a screenshot or save any of the images. Sure enough, the website was taken down the day before her presentation, and Jenny had to scramble to find and analyze a new example. You can save screenshots of websites in an online references manager program like Zotero or in your own filing system (see Chapter 7 for file storage and sharing tips).

Collecting Assets

As you are creating a plan for your multimodal project, whether that's a storyboard, script, mock-up, outline, or other form of prewriting/designing (see Chapter 7 for more ideas on drafting), you'll want to make sure you create a source and asset list to help you keep your ideas in one place. You are likely familiar with source lists, more commonly referred to as works cited lists or bibliographies. (We'll talk more about those in a later section of this chapter, Citing Assets and Sources, on pp. 158–64.) A well-organized multimodal project also includes an asset list. Asset lists, like the one the Touchpoints in this chapter have you build, help you keep track of the items you are using in your project and can help you think through why you're using those items in the first place. It can also help in creating the final bibliography. An asset list will generally include two kinds of assets: repurposed and created.

Repurposed assets are those you didn't create yourself and are borrowing from other authors (with their permission), such as screenshots, found images, prerecorded sound or movie clips, quotations from written sources, and so on. For the repurposed assets, consider the following questions:

- Where is the asset coming from, and do you have permission and/or is it ethical to use it? (We talk more about permissions later in this chapter.) Include any source information so you can easily go back later and find the asset again if you need to.

- How will you get the asset from its original location to your project files? What technologies might you need to make that conversion/relocation happen?

Created assets are those you make yourself to use in your project, such as by shooting original video, recording sound, taking photos, writing text, designing logos, and so on. For created assets, consider the following questions that impact your multimodal composition process:

- What hardware (cameras, sound recording equipment, markers, paper) and software (sound or video editing software, photo manipulation programs, etc.) do you need access to in order to create and edit your assets?

- How much time will it take to create these assets for your project? As with any project, especially projects using digital technology, remember that you will almost certainly need some extra time to troubleshoot.

For both types of assets, you should also ask these questions:

- How will any particular asset help you convey the purpose of your project? What is its individual purpose within the larger project context?

- Why are you choosing a particular asset genre or medium over another? (For instance, why choose this sound clip instead of another sound clip? Or, why choose this sound clip instead of an image?)

For example, writer/designer Courteney created an asset list for a video she made to analyze action movies. Most of her video would consist of created assets. She decided to break down her created asset column to include both "needs" (the assets and other materials she needs to create for her project) and "solutions" (how she imagines she will get these assets). Working from this table, Courteney made sure her room was ready, asked her actor friends for help in advance, and made sure the camera's battery was charged well before she set out to film anything.

Courteney's Assets Chart

Needs	Solutions
Bedroom setting	Use my bedroom when roommate is in class.
Narrator (actress)	Me; wear motorcycle jacket
Muse (actress)	Sarah, my friend in the theater department
Release form for actress	Get a sample copy from instructor; print out before filming with Sarah.
Video camera	Check this out from the school library (what are its hours?).
Video editing program	I can't use the Mac lab at school because I work during open hours, so I'll use my laptop, which has Quicktime on it.

⊙— **Touchpoint: Building an Asset List**

If you're not already at work on a multimodal project, imagine you've been asked to create a flyer advertising an event of your choice happening at your college (a sporting event, department lecture, reading series, etc.). These flyers will be put up both on campus and in local community establishments (coffee shops, grocery stores, restaurants, etc.). Make a rough sketch of what you want your flyer to look like so as to help you think through what assets you will need.

Now, create an asset list that will help you gather the items you need to write/ design the flyer. Or, if you're already working on a multimodal assignment, create an asset list for your project. For your list, design two sections: one for created assets, and one for repurposed assets. Make sure each asset has its own row, then create a column for each of the bulleted questions listed in the Collecting Assets section (pp. 146–47). Use the questions there to guide you as you fill in your table.

If you are working on a large-scale multimodal project, the Touchpoints throughout this chapter will ask you to return to this list and add to it. To accommodate that work, you may want to create a table that includes assets listed in each row and the summary/descriptions requested as column headers.

Working with Multimodal Sources

Working with multimodal sources and assets often requires strategies for collecting, citing, and sharing that are different from the research processes you may be familiar with. This section will discuss how to find credible sources for your project. As a reminder, sources are texts, such as books, articles, websites, and so on, that you can use to gather information about a topic or genre.

Find Credible Sources

Every kind of text has a point to make and some type of argument it wants to get across, even if it's just to persuade the reader to pay attention to the information presented. For this reason, you need to think strategically about your sources. No matter what type of multimodal project you create—whether it's a promotional flyer, an informational website, a family scrapbook, or an annual report—you should ask yourself what kinds of sources, information, and evidence will be the most convincing to the audience you are trying to reach. That being said, in an era of fake news, it is import- ant to make sure the material you use isn't just convincing but also

"On the Internet, nobody knows you're a dog."

Figure 6.2 Credible Sources Make You Credible

Think about how fake news sources build fake credibility so that audiences come to trust their knowledge and character. What can you do as a critical reader to spot these moves?

Peter Steiner/CartoonStock.com

ethically sourced and accurate (which can be done by following guidelines both on pp. 146–47 and pp. 149–51).

In all rhetorical situations, authors need to consider how best to build their credibility so that audiences trust their knowledge and character. This credibility is called *ethos*. Using credible and reliable sources is one of the most common ways of building ethos, and you've probably used this tactic when writing traditional research papers for which you were required to draw on scholarly sources, such as books and journal articles. That kind of source material can be equally useful in multimodal projects, but you can also build ethos by having a well-designed project that pays attention to *how* the text works, as well as *why* it works the way it does, as we discussed in Chapter 3. And the design comes not only from creating your own multimodal content but also from finding outside multimodal sources or assets (such as images, sound clips, Web templates, screenshots, photos, line drawings, and graphs) that can lend credibility to your project. (And for the record, scholars also produce "scholarly" texts beyond books and journal articles, such as the webtexts used in many examples throughout this book.)

Evaluate Sources

The following are some questions you can use to evaluate whether your potential multimodal sources are credible. Some of the questions may be more important than others for your project. Remember that the credibility of sources will depend on your answers to the kinds of questions we have listed (so make sure you can answer those questions in relation to each choice) and *also* on the rhetorical situation and genre of the text you are producing.

- **How do you define credibility in relation to your project goals?** What makes a source credible can differ from project to project. For many projects, for example, a source is made more credible by having a known author. However, if you were composing a project about the human impacts of natural disaster, the inclusion of film or video footage shot by an unknown author in an affected area could prove to be highly persuasive to your target audience. The credibility of a particular source depends on your argument and the rhetorical situation for your text.

- **What is the purpose of your source? Does it seem biased in any way?** Is the purpose of the source to persuade? Does it seem evenhanded? Is it limited to one point of view? If so, should this affect your use of the source? Sometimes it might even strengthen your argument to use sources that are overtly biased, especially if your point is to illustrate how people with different perspectives think or act on a particular issue.

- **What information can you find about the text's creator and/or publisher?** Are the author's or organization's qualifications listed? If not, are they well known? Your audience's familiarity with or preconceptions about the author of a source can influence their response to your argument. For example, a video clip from a national news outlet like the *New York Times* may seem more credible to some audiences than others. How can you account for the bias of your intended audience in selecting sources when you might need to persuade them of something they don't already agree with?

- **Have you seen this author or organization referred to in any of your other sources?** A source that is quoted or referenced frequently by other sources is generally one that authors and audiences find useful, whether it's to highlight their credibility and lend evidence to a topic or to critique the original author and purpose.

- **Is the information believable?** Why or why not? Consider also what type of person might find the information unbelievable. For example, if you need a source that explains the Second Amendment, a video that was made by a gun shop owner will have a much different impact on audiences than a video made by a constitutional lawyer.

- **What medium is the source?** Researchers have found that visual evidence (like photos or videos) makes information more believable to audiences, but some audiences may question whether a visual is undoctored. Consider which media will be most credible for your project.

- **Are your sources diverse and inclusive?** Sometimes authors overlook diversity when considering sources, and this can affect the credibility of their text with audiences. Considering diversity and difference reminds us to analyze our audiences and to remember that we always have something new to learn from others. Make sure you aren't interviewing only your friends for an oral history project or choosing to represent only one gender or one race in a project that requires discussion of multiple cultures. Don't try to speak for a population that can speak for itself.

⦿— Touchpoint: Annotating Credible Sources in an Asset List

If you are in the process of writing/designing a multimodal project for class, create a list in which you annotate each source you intend to use for your project. If you are not in that process or that stage, choose a recent assignment from any class and create a list in which you annotate each source you used. Where possible, the list should include the following elements:

- **The source's metadata.** Document enough information about the site—including author, title, publication venue, and Web address, if relevant—so that you, your collaborators, or your instructor can go back and find the source.

- **A summary of the source.** Describe the source's medium and give a brief description of the source's content. For example, if you're using a website about Cuban Do-It-Yourself (DIY) practices as a source to understand how different cultures engage with technology, you might describe how the website uses persuasive modes and media to make that point.

- **A description of the asset and its metadata from that source.** For example, if you want to use an image from the Cuban DIY website, you'll want to describe the asset briefly: What kind of image is it? What is it about? Who is its author (if different from the whole site)? What is its Web address, filename, and/or title?

- **A description of how the source or asset relates to your project,** including any important/major issues it discusses that you can use to support your project idea or any important/major issues the source or asset leaves out that your project covers.

Copyright Issues and Ethics

As you search for credible sources and rhetorically appropriate assets for your project, be aware of some ethical issues associated with collecting assets that don't belong to you. The majority of ethical issues we'll address in this section relate to copyright law; those issues include the fair-use principle, obtaining permissions, and the use of copyrighted material that authors have purposely given others more freedom to use under certain Creative Commons designations. While avoiding legal trouble is certainly a good reason to pay attention to copyright issues, it is also just good practice to honor the work of the writer/designers who came before you and composed the texts you are now repurposing.

Copyright

Copyright is a legal device that gives the creator of a text the right to control how that text can be used. For a work to be copyrighted, the United States Copyright Office demands that it meet the following criteria:

1. **Originality.** The work must be an original creation—though it's not really as simple as that because a work that is an adaptation or a transformation of a previous work can be copyrighted.

2. **Fixity.** The work must be capable of being stored in some way. An unrecorded speech cannot be copyrighted; once the speech is written down or videotaped, however, it can be copyrighted.

3. **Minimal creativity.** This category is subjective, but for the most part anything that includes some original work will be eligible for copyright protection. Very short works such as your name, phone numbers, and recipes can't be copyrighted, however, because the amount of creativity required to formulate any of those types of texts is considered to be too minimal. In other words, under copyright law, "creativity" is considered to take some effort. How *much* effort is often a matter for lawyers and judges to decide.

The point of copyright is to give authors control over how their text is used. Authors are the only ones who can legally distribute and/or sell their work—in short, they are the only ones who should be able to profit from it. The moment an author "fixes" an original idea into a text, they immediately have copyright over that text, unless

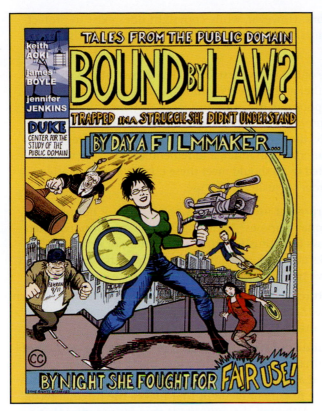

Figure 6.3 *Tales from the Public Domain*

Some works—usually very old ones—aren't covered by copyright. These fall into what's known as the public domain. For more information on public domain, read the comic *Bound by Law?* at http://law.duke.edu/cspd/comics/.

Courtesy James Boyle

the author signs the rights over to another person or to a group such as a publishing company.

When you're composing a multimodal project, copyright needs to be a prime consideration. As you'll learn in the next section, some of your assets may fall under the guidelines for fair use, but if you ever plan to share your project, make sure that you observe general copyright principles. Sometimes it's easy to forget about copyright because of how simple it is to find images or songs through a quick Web search. But just because you find a source online doesn't mean that it is copyright-free.

Fair Use

Having to consider copyright law for your multimodal project may feel as though your creativity is being limited, but you need to remember that copyright exists in large part to protect an author's original work—and you are probably quite protective of your own work. However, while copyright does exist to protect original authors, the fair-use doctrine limits an author's total control.

The principle of fair use was established to allow authors to use portions of other authors' texts without permission for educational, nonprofit, reportorial, or critical purposes. Anyone working on a multimodal project should pay attention to the rules of fair use. Unfortunately, those rules aren't always clear-cut. But keep the following four criteria in mind, and remember that your usage of the copyrighted work should meet these criteria as stringently as possible in order to qualify as fair use:

1. **The purpose of use.** Is the work being used for nonprofit or educational purposes? Is it being used for criticism, commentary, news reporting, teaching, scholarship, or research? Fair use looks more favorably on texts that meet these criteria and that have transformed the original work into a new use.

2. **The nature of the copyrighted work.** Is it factual? Has it been published? Fair use favors factual published works over unpublished works or forms of artistic expression.

3. **The amount of the work used.** The smaller the portion of the original text you use, the more likely this use is to be protected as fair use, unless you borrow the "heart" of the work, the feature or element that makes the original recognizable. (Although the opposite is true for parodies that require borrowing from and building on the heart of the work.)

4. **The market effect of the use.** Will your reuse affect the market value or sales of the original text? Work excerpted for educational or scholarly purposes often doesn't affect the market value of the original, so this question is good to ask in tandem with the others in this list.

Amelia, Hailey, and Kaylee, three of Kristin's students, were working on a rhetorical genre analysis for class. They made a five-minute video analyzing billboards that focused on environmental issues. Because they used screenshots from the different billboards and organizational websites, they had to think about copyright. They were pretty certain their screenshots of billboards from Coca-Cola, the Sierra Club, and the Michigan Department of Environment, Great Lakes, and Energy (see **Fig. 6.4**) fell under fair use for several reasons:

1. The texts would be used for educational purposes—specifically, for criticism and analysis (**purpose of use**).

Figure 6.4 Screenshot from Hailey, Kaylee, and Amelia's Genre Analysis Video

Notice that we aren't showing the billboard they used from Coca-Cola, because even though their use of it constituted fair use in the context of the classroom, our use of it in this textbook would not fall under fair use and we would have to pay for copyright permissions. Fair use changes depending on context!

2. The billboards and websites themselves had already been published (**nature of copyrighted work**).

3. The text would be available only to other people in their class (**small market effect of use**).

While it is often the case that most of your work for class will fall under fair use given the criteria we've discussed, it is important to think through how you are using your sources and assets so that you protect yourself from any legal trouble, as well as honor the writer/designers of the texts you incorporate.

Permissions

In many cases, if you want to use part of a copyrighted text in your own multimodal project, you are supposed to request permission from the copyright owner. In some cases, this might be as simple as sending an email or a letter to a friendly author, who will grant you written permission to use the text for your project. On the other hand, getting permission from some copyright holders can be overly complicated, expensive, and potentially unnecessary (depending on whether your use of the material is fair). For instance, Courteney, an author who was composing a video-based analysis of action films and who wanted to cite scenes from *The Dark Knight* and other Hollywood movies in her project (see p. 147), discovered that she would have to fill out a lengthy permission form supplied by the films' production company, Warner Brothers, and include a proposal explaining her use of each clip from each Warner Brothers movie. In addition, Courteney would not have been able to use or edit any clips from these movies without first getting approval and (most likely) paying a fee.

Most DIY multimodal projects (like the kind we discuss in this book) don't have a budget, so the actions of requesting permission and paying for the use of clips can raise more ethical and economic issues than they solve. That's when we encourage you to exercise your fair-use rights, transforming an asset for your project by critiquing or studying it for academic purposes, parodying it (among other appropriate fair uses), or using more permissions-friendly clips from a Creative Commons or similar search (discussed in the next section).

When Humans Are the Text

You may need a different kind of permission if you are interviewing a person about their personal attitudes, beliefs, experiences, and the like. Most organizations (institutions of higher learning, in particular) require you to have your project approved by the local institutional review board (IRB) if the project involves research that experiments on people or asks personal questions of people, *and* if you plan on making the project public. IRBs exist to make sure that certain research—in this case, human subjects research—is conducted ethically. That being said, the IRB process doesn't absolve you of all ethical responsibility. If you are working with interviews or any community-engaged research, ask your instructor for resources on doing this work responsibly.

For a film that she planned to show only in class (a use that is *not* considered public), Courteney needed another kind of permission: the permission of the actor she wanted to film. She could have requested a signed consent form from the actor or obtained vocal permission recorded on film. If people are recognizable in your footage, you need their permission.

Creative Commons

Confused or frustrated about copyright, fair use, and permissions? Look into Creative Commons (CC), a nonprofit organization devoted to giving authors more control over how their work is used. CC also provides researchers with a massive collection of assets that are easily searchable and that can be used without worrying about strict copyright laws, ensuring fair use, or asking (and paying) for permissions. Authors can choose from six licenses, each of which is some combination of the following:

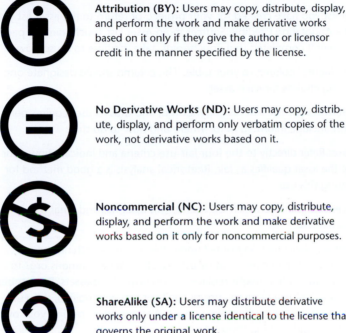

Attribution (BY): Users may copy, distribute, display, and perform the work and make derivative works based on it only if they give the author or licensor credit in the manner specified by the license.

No Derivative Works (ND): Users may copy, distribute, display, and perform only verbatim copies of the work, not derivative works based on it.

Noncommercial (NC): Users may copy, distribute, display, and perform the work and make derivative works based on it only for noncommercial purposes.

ShareAlike (SA): Users may distribute derivative works only under a license identical to the license that governs the original work.

Creative Commons. Made available by Creative Commons Attribution 4.0 International license.

A text licensed with an Attribution-Noncommercial (BY-NC) license can be used in your noncommercial project as long as you give the original author credit. The other great thing about Creative Commons is that you can license your own work after you've completed your project. (If you use any CC assets with the ShareAlike designation, you *must* apply a Creative Commons ShareAlike license to your project.)

When creating your project, you'll want to think about

- What kind of license might work best for you. Remember, if you don't apply a CC license to your work, it will automatically fall under copyright protection.

- What your stakeholders want. Discuss with stakeholders which kind of license your project might need. If your project is primarily for your classmates and teacher, consider how and why a CC license might be helpful. Make a note of which license would be best for your project and why.

⊙— **Touchpoint: Tracking Copyright and CC-Licensed Work**

Use an asset list you have created for your project, or return to the asset list you started in the Annotating Credible Sources in an Asset List Touchpoint on page 151. If you haven't completed that Touchpoint, take the time to do so now.

Next, add a "Rights" column to your table. The column should designate one of the following choices for each asset:

- **Get permission:** The asset is copyrighted, and thus its use requires permission. Include information for where and how to do that.

- **Fair use:** Refer directly to the four fair-use criteria and indicate how your use of the asset qualifies as fair. Rhetorical analysis is a good method for indicating this use.

- **CC-licensed:** Indicate which CC license this asset has and what uses the license allows.

For any assets you have that do not fall under fair use, try searching the Creative Commons-licensed assets at http://search.creativecommons.org/ to find additional sources that might replace those copyrighted assets. Remember to look for assets that can be used commercially or can be modified, if these needs are relevant to your multimodal project. Also consider creating your own original assets instead of using those of others.

Citing Assets and Sources

Strict citation rules such as those of the Modern Language Association (MLA) and the American Psychological Association (APA) often are difficult to use when you're producing multimodal projects. This is because those guides were created primarily for print-based scholarship, such as essays, articles, and class papers. You *might* use MLA, APA, or some other citation style in your multimodal project, but that will depend entirely on your genre and rhetorical situation. See **Figure 6.5** for an example of a social media post citation.

In this book, we have only two rules for citations:

1. Provide enough information about each source so that readers can find it themselves.

2. Use a citation style that is credible within the context of the genre you've chosen to produce.

Figure 6.5 How to Cite a Social Media Post

Social media posts, whether TikToks or Insta stories, can (and should!) be cited. This image from artist and Professor Dylan Miner was posted on Instagram and can be cited in APA style as: Miner, D. [@wiisaakodewinini]. (2020, January 3). *Capitalism cannot be reformed and the Earth cannot be replaced* [Digital image]. Instagram. https://www.instagram.com/p/CJmx9tDlFmt/.

Dylan Miner

Why these two rules? Because attributing your sources shows that you care about your readers, your text, and the authors whose work you're using, which helps readers interpret and even sympathize with your argument—not to mention that it helps with your credibility.

Different style guides call your source list different things. You are likely already familiar, as a student, with the type of source list called a bibliography. The MLA style guide calls the same type of source list a works cited list. The APA style guide calls it a references list. A film or other media project would call it credits. What you call your list of citations (if you even have or need a list of all the citations in your project) will depend on what genre your project is.

Provide Enough Information for Readers

It's infuriating when someone you trust shares a link to an image on Twitter or via text without including any additional context, and the link turns out to be "404 Not Found"—that is, a dead end. In that situation, you might ask your friend for more information (if you cared enough to follow up), launch an image search of the entire Internet for the correct image, and then sort through the 427,000 hits to find an image that you *think* is the one your friend sent you. To avoid creating this sort of frustration, you should provide enough information so that readers will be able to find your sources or will at least know that you attributed your sources well enough to give credit where credit is due. And they'll like you for that.

Here are a few basic questions to help you credit your sources:

- Where is the source's home?
- What is its address?
- What is its name?
- Who is its owner?
- When was it born?

(Yes, it's sort of like finding the home of a lost puppy.)

Let's ask these questions about the screenshot in **Figure 6.7.**

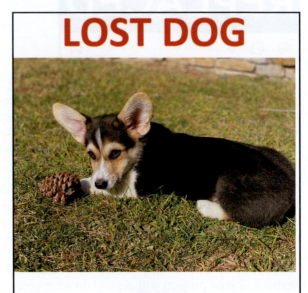

Figure 6.6 Finding Missing Things

Courtesy of Jennifer Sheppard

Figure 6.7 Piled Higher and Deeper (PhD) by Jorge Cham

"Piled Higher and Deeper" by Jorge Cham, www.phdcomics.com

First of all, what is this asset's **home** and **address**? Let's say you ran across this image on Facebook and didn't know what it was, but you had a link you could click on so that you could read it in the context of the original site. You'd follow the link, which is the image's address (http://www.phdcomics.com/comics/archive .php?comicid=405), and from there you could discover the rest of the missing information. The asset's home is the website the comic lives on, called *Piled Higher and Deeper*. Note that the address of a Web asset is usually *not* the same thing as the main page (the main page in this case would be http://www.phdcomics.com/comics.php). For the purpose of citation, a main page is like the street name of a lost puppy's home—close, but not quite enough information to get the cute little thing back to its owners. So make sure you get the specific Web address, not just the main page address.

What is the image's name? In this case, it's the comic's title. In many websites, the title of a text that is part of a collection will be listed at the top of the browser, along with the collection's name. If the title is not listed at the top, study the page to see if you can figure out what the title is. In this image, the name appears in capital letters on the comic itself: "Deciphering Academese."

Now, who owns this cute little thing? On a website that's designed like a blog or Tumblr, the author may not be readily evident, so search for links with words like *About* or *Author*, or look for a copyright note, which is where we find Jorge Cham's name. Cham is the owner of this comic. (Note that when you don't have the author's full name, you can use their handle—for example, s2ceball.)

Finally, on blog-like websites such as this one, each post is usually tagged with the publication date, otherwise known as the birth date. In this case, the publication date is January 18, 2004. Now we have enough information to track down the asset again, if we need to, and we can use the name, owner, birth date, home, and address to create a citation.

Use a Credible Citation Style for Your Genre

This is usually the point in the production cycle where the MLA or APA style guide or *The Chicago Manual of Style* (*CMOS* or Chicago) gets pulled out—or a website that has examples of these citation styles gets pulled up. But for your multimodal project, you can't assume that you'll use MLA, APA, or Chicago style. Instead, you need to consider what citation styles look like *in the genre* that meets your rhetorical needs. Here's an easy example: when you go to the movies, the soundtrack credits don't appear in MLA style at the end. Readers have come to expect that the sound citations in a movie will follow the format shown in **Figure 6.8**. When you use this style in a movie, it makes your citations credible, professional, and easily recognizable by your audience.

FEEL FLOWS
Written by
John Rieley & Carl Wilson
Performed by The Beach Boys
Courtesy of Capitol Records
Under license from EMI-Capitol
Music Special Markets

FEVER DOG
Written by Russell Hammond
Performed by Stillwater

EVERY PICTURE
TELLS A STORY
Written by
Rod Stewart & Ron Wood
Performed by Rod Stewart
Courtesy of

RIVER
Written & Performed by
Joni Mitchell
Courtesy of Reprise Records
By arrangement with
Warner Special Products

SWEET LEAF
Written by Frank Iommi,
William Ward, Terence Butler
& John Osbourne
Performed by Black Sabbath
Courtesy of Downlane Limited

SMALL TIME BLUES
Written & Performed by
Pete Droge

Figure 6.8 **Music Credits in a Film**
DreamWorks/Photofest

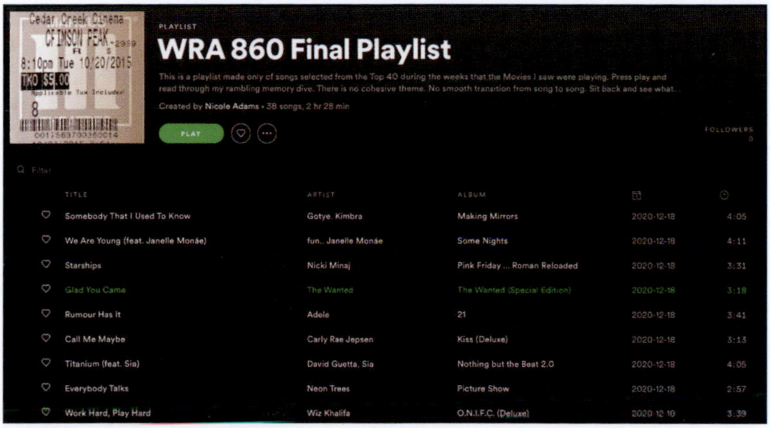

Figure 6.9 Spotify Playlist

Courtesy of Nicole Adams

Consider also the genre conventions of the streaming music playlist. No matter what streaming service you may use, listeners expect to see a title for the playlist, often an image or icon associated with the playlist, a description, and then the track list itself. The track list usually includes song title, artist name, album name, and often the length of the track itself. **Figure 6.9** shows a playlist Nicole Adams made for a multimodal class project on curation and memory. Nicole wrote/designed a blog that included pictures and stories of movie stubs she has collected over the years. She then curated this playlist comprised of songs from the Top 40 during the weeks the movies were playing. Nicole asked Kristin, her professor, to listen to this playlist while reading/viewing the blog. This multimodal experience not only brought together a range of modes, it also shared the genre convention of the streaming music playlist.

Touchpoint: Finding and Citing Sources

Figure 6.10 is a screenshot from a webtext (a scholarly, multimedia article) published in the online journal *Kairos*. Locate the original webtext and create a citation appropriate for the genre of multimodal project you're working on.

You can also apply this practice to the rest of your assets in your multimodal project, using the Assets List you created (or will now create) in the Tracking Copyright and CC-Licensed Work Touchpoint on page 158. Add a "Citations" column to your assets list. This is where you will decide how your assets will be cited in your final project. Look to other texts similar to the multimodal project you're working on and see how they include citation information. Remember our two rules for citations: provide enough information about each source so that readers can find it themselves, and use a citation style that is credible within the context of the genre you've chosen to produce.

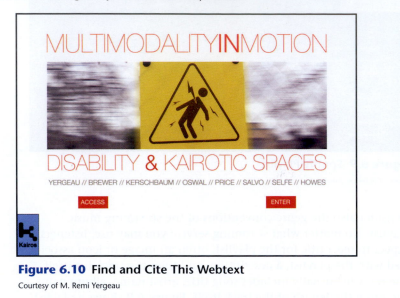

Figure 6.10 Find and Cite This Webtext
Courtesy of M. Remi Yergeau

Organizing and Sharing Assets

In our digital age, we often put stuff online and then forget about it. We don't have a good plan to archive things, which may be fine for Snapchats and random photos. But if you're working for a client or even doing a class project, you may need to keep copies of your work or ensure that you have continued access to it for years to come. For instance, you might need to create a project portfolio to get a job or woo future clients. So consider where you might keep, and how you might organize, copies of everything you make, in case the hosting site you're using goes bankrupt.

If you're working in a group, or even if you're working alone but across multiple computers in a lab, at work, or at home, you'll need to find a good way to share your multimodal assets. Using a USB flash drive or an external hard drive can work in some cases—except when you lose the drive, forget to bring it with you, drop it, or try to save files on it that are too big. Online cloud storage sites are a great alternative. These sites allow you to register (sometimes for free) and save files remotely on their Internet servers so that you can access the files from any other computer, smartphone, or netbook connected to the Internet. These sites are usually password-protected, so you can back up your private files online (although the sites do come with security risks, so don't upload all your banking information!), and you can share project-based folders with anyone you are collaborating with. Examples of these sites include Dropbox, Google Drive, and Box.

No matter what type of sharing system you use, it's good practice to name and organize your files and folders clearly. Doing so will help you find items and keep track of which assets you've already edited, and it will also help other users collaborate, edit, or revise your project later, whether or not you're available. In this section, you'll find some tips for naming, organizing, and sharing your assets. These tips are specific to certain kinds of media files. For instance, avoiding spaces and punctuation in filenames is useful when producing multimodal projects in certain kinds of technological systems (websites, audio files, etc.) but not as important with other types of systems (presentation software like Prezi or blogging platforms like WordPress). Although following a standard set of guidelines will ensure that your final project will work across all software and media types, you do have some flexibility in managing your assets, depending on the genre, technology, and media you're using or producing.

Categorize Your Files Appropriately

Creating folders will help you keep your assets organized and will help you find them again when you need them, just as keeping your clothes organized in a dresser or on shelves makes it easier to get dressed in the morning. Most effective folder structures are arranged in a hierarchy, with the broadest categories at the top, and with the categories getting progressively more detailed as they go down.

Follow these suggestions for using a folder structure to keep your assets organized:

- **Keep all of your project files in one place.** Some software programs require you to keep the files in a specific location. Research the requirements of your chosen software program and follow its instructions.

- **Create a folder structure** that will be easy to maintain throughout the design and revision process.

  Take a look at the example in **Figure 6.11**. This multimodal book review appeared in the online journal *Kairos*. On the root

Figure 6.11
File Structure
of a Web-Based
Book Review

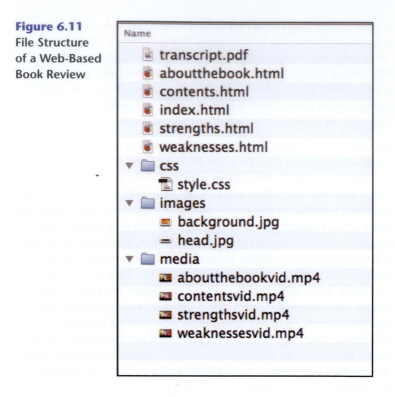

(or main) folder level are the .html files and then folders for .css files, images, and media. Notice how there are no spaces or capital letters in this file structure and how each folder's name clearly indicates which assets it will include.

- **Name your files and folders** according to what they *are* and what they *do*. If you're using multiple images, sound clips, and videos, you might create three folders called *images*, *sound*, and *video*. (See the discussion of naming conventions in the following section.)

- **Create a separate folder for editable files** that won't go in the final project (we call these *working files*).

Use Good Naming Conventions

Certain types of technologies, such as the Web, rely on exact characters to find files. For example, if you save an .html page as "PuPPies.html," you will find it in a Web browser only by typing the exact filename—that is, *not* "Puppies.html" or "puPPies.html." If you can't remember whether you capitalized the first (or second or

Figure 6.12 Be Careful When Naming Something "Final"

"Piled Higher and Deeper" by Jorge Cham, www.phdcomics.com

third) letter, then you won't be able to find your file. Here are some best practices for naming files:

- **Use all lowercase letters in filenames.** If you know that you use all lowercase letters without exception, then you'll know to (1) name the file "puppies.html" and (2) look for "puppies. html" in your Web browser.

- **Use hyphens (-) or underscores (_) instead of spaces.** Web browsers and some multimedia editing programs can't read spaces, and/or they will translate them to a "%20" symbol (which nobody can understand), so it's best to avoid spaces entirely (as in the filename "student-interviews10-11 .mov").

- **Be brief and informative.** Instead of naming an image "red_butterfly_on_fence_in_spring.jpg," consider using "red_ butterfly.jpg" as the filename. Or simply call it "butterfly.jpg" if this is your only image of a butterfly.

Use Version Control

You will likely compile multiple versions of your assets throughout your project. For instance, you'll need to crop that audio track from two minutes to ten seconds. If you are exchanging files or using an online, shared repository such as Dropbox, using version control is especially important so that you don't accidentally save over a revised version, causing you to lose new work.

- **If you plan to include dates in your filenames, decide as a group what date format you will use.** Will it be MM_DD_YYYY (for example, "clip1_10_23_2011.mov") or MM_DD_YY? Dates in filenames are OK, but everyone on your team needs to use them in a consistent manner.

- **Use an online version control system.** Git, Subversion, Mercurial, and the like (some are free) automatically assign versions to your project files. Using these can be a little more complicated than just naming a file, but they will ensure that there is no confusion among versions, particularly if you are collaborating on different stages of a project. They also provide cloud-based backups of your work.

◉— Touchpoint: Getting Your Assets in Order

We cannot stress enough the importance of organizing your working files! Without taking proper care to manage your assets and sources, you might start making duplicates or accidentally overwriting your only versions.

Using the sections in this chapter, complete the following checklist to create a clean and rhetorically understandable working environment. Even if you're creating an analog project with analog assets, such as a scrapbook or poster, you can apply these principles through methods such as clearly labeling manila folders for different kinds of assets and working through paper-based mock-ups before using your only color copy of a photograph in your final draft.

- ❑ Create a system of tracking copyright and sharing assets with your project team or stakeholders (pp. 152–58 and pp. 164–65)
- ❑ Categorize your files (pp. 165–66)
- ❑ Apply appropriate filenaming conventions (pp. 166–67)
- ❑ Set up a system for version control (p. 168)

Working with Technologies

7

You have an idea of the *what* and the *how* of your project. You've found sources that can help you get started. Now it's time to think about the practical steps you will take to start building your project. This chapter covers some possibilities for designing multimodal projects and asks you to consider the affordances offered by various analog and digital technologies. (For more on affordances, see Understanding Modes, Media, and Affordances in Chapter 1, pp. 22–27.) In addition to thinking about projects that create brand new content, you can also think about ways of repurposing existing or found artifacts. That is, your project might be a mix of original content created by you, plus assets, such as images or video clips found on YouTube, that you integrate and relate to your rhetorical situation. The sections here complement the projects you will create in the Write/Design! activities in Part One. Because your choice of media and technologies will change depending on your rhetorical situation, you might use different parts of this chapter from what your classmates use—that's OK! Figure out what makes sense for your project and purpose, then use the information in this chapter that supports your design.

Choosing How to Work with Technologies

When it comes to building a multimodal project, there are hundreds of technology options to choose from. Any number of technologies may work best for your *current* project, but next month you might be working on a completely different project that needs a totally different piece of technology, so we can't just say, "Use WordPress!" or "Learn Audacity!" Instead, we offer suggestions for *learning how to learn* which technologies might be most useful for you in any given writing situation. With new technologies emerging every day, as well as constant updates to the applications we already use, learning how to learn about the new affordances and constraints these offer is a critical skill.

People who excel at integrating new approaches and technologies often have the following mindset:

- **An openness to seeking help from a variety of sources.** People who embrace this mindset are generally unafraid to ask questions of experienced users and spend time searching for and using diverse sources of help. These might include print manuals, online tutorials, YouTube videos, conversations with colleagues, discussion forums, tech support via email or chat, and in-application help.

- **A positive attitude towards change.** Rather than dreading the process of learning how to integrate a new process or use a new tool, these people focus on the benefits of their efforts to learn and adapt. They seek out new applications or new versions of older ones to capitalize on improved features.

- **Curiosity.** Rather than making a snap judgment about a new idea or tool, people who use their curiosity to ask questions and to explore possibilities of new features tend to take fuller advantage of new affordances.

- **Vulnerability and a willingness to take risks.** Meaningful learning often takes place when people experiment and try out new possibilities. Often, these early attempts aren't fully successful, but they allow learners to see elements that work, problem areas that need more development, and hypotheses about how to proceed more productively the next time. People with this mindset don't see these attempts as failures but as chances to learn through doing.

- **A commitment to problem-solving.** Instead of seeing problems as insurmountable roadblocks, people who think critically and creatively about alternatives are actively learning about approaches that will help them proceed. Some of the best solutions come from trying out new approaches or adapting old ones to fit the new affordances.

◉— Touchpoint: Learning How to Learn

With these strategies and characteristics of successful writer/designers in mind, make a list of your personal approaches to learning new software, applications, or updates. What sites or discussion forums do you rely on? Do you use printed materials, and if so, which ones and why? Do you prefer textual, visual, or audio instructions, or some combination? What factors influence your choices, and why? What is one new method for learning you could try in your current project?

Deciding Between Analog and Digital

One essential choice in planning your project is whether it should be in analog or digital format. Remember that your multimodal project doesn't have to be digital. Perhaps you'll be delivering your multimodal project on posterboard at a student research showcase or a community meeting, or as a flyer tacked to the office bulletin board or campus event board in the student center. However, even if you're planning to deliver your project on paper or in person, you may still need to gather digital assets and use digital technologies to produce it; for example, you may want to use InDesign to create a printed brochure, or Canva to design a flyer for bulletin boards across your campus.

But what if you were to choose both? **Figure 7.1** shows a slide from a student team's digital PowerPoint presentation on the Chicano Park Memorial Murals in San Diego, California. **Figure 7.2** shows a print/analog handout the team used to support the message of their on-screen presentation. It contains a photo and short description of each mural they discussed in their presentation. This is an example of a project team choosing both analog and digital texts for their rhetorical situation.

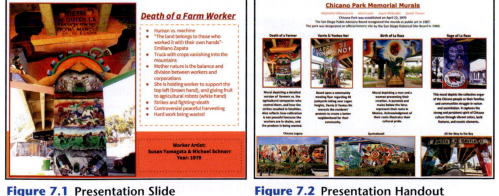

Figure 7.1 **Presentation Slide**
Courtesy Alejandra Villavicienco, Joyce Melendez, Alicia Leon, Sarah Tanori

Figure 7.2 **Presentation Handout**
Courtesy Alejandra Villavicienco, Joyce Melendez, Alicia Leon, Sarah Tanori

What Does Your Audience Need?

Not all of the questions listed here will apply to your project, but they might help you think through the entire production process—from idea to use—in more concrete terms so that your project planning won't encounter too many surprises or obstacles. The questions here are meant to prompt ideas.

- Who are the primary users or audience members of your project? What are they like? How can you research to find out more information about them?

- What modes and media should you use to reach them? Do you have any restrictions on the technical or media forms of your project? (For example, are you required to make a flyer, an app, a podcast?)

- Where will your audience get access to your project? What is the viewing context? Will your audience look at a print or analog copy of your project, an online version, or an electronic file stored in the cloud or on an external drive? If your project has digital components, you may need to research the file-size limitations of online hosting sites. If your project is analog, consider its physical size (or weight) and how it will be used in the location in which it's made and where it will be used—for example, how will you get it from one location to another?

- Should access to your project be restricted to your audience or client, or should it be available to people who may not be part of your intended audience? When you upload a video to YouTube, for example, you can set it to be viewable by any user or restrict access to just the people you share the link with. Are you allowed to share, based on permissions or confidentiality issues?

- Will your audience need any special hardware or software to view/use your project? For example, if you created a webtext in HTML/CSS, any Web browser will be able to display the files. But if you design for a desktop platform, your project might not render properly on a mobile phone. How will you make sure that your audience has the right technical setup? For analog projects, such as a poster presentation, how will it be attached to a display stand or wall? Which area of a room or building will provide the best viewing area for your audience, given traffic patterns and possible crowds? And who provides the stand? The tape? What kind of tape do you need to secure it properly?

- Is your project platform-dependent? Some programs export file types that are viewable only on a single platform, such as a Mac or PC. How will your audience gain access to the platform they need to view your project? Or can you create the project in multiple file types? What file format should you save your project in so that your audience can most easily access it? For example, if you've created an audio project, have you exported your final version as an MP3 so that it can be played on a wide variety of computers and devices? If you want to supplement your digital files with analog accompaniments, will there be a place to display printouts, flyers, or brochures so that your audience will be sure to see them? If your project needs to be printed, have you provided the printer with the correct file type?

- What resolution or compression quality should you use given the final project genre and medium? If you are producing materials for print, their resolution should be a minimum of 300 PPI (pixels per inch). If you're creating a video that you want to be viewable on the Web, you'll need to carefully balance image quality with file size so that users can start to watch the video as quickly as possible but still see clear images.

The choice of media and technology is highly dependent on the primary audience's needs within the rhetorical situation of your project. These questions are meant to help you make these choices with your project team early in the hands-on design process so that you will have a successful transition from the proposal stage to rough cut and rough draft. We go in depth with some of the technology choices in the next section, Assessing Technological Affordances (pp. 174–78), so read ahead if you want to consider project type in relation to technological affordances before doing the Touchpoint activity that follows.

⊙— Touchpoint: **Choosing an Analog or Digital Project**

Imagine you're planning your own multimedia presentation with an accompanying handout for members of the audience. Brainstorm a pitch or plan for the presentation components, considering questions like the following:

- What is the subject and purpose of the presentation?

- What information should go in the presentation, and what should go in the handout?

- For the presentation component, what technologies will you use? What assets will you include? You'll probably want to choose a technology designed for this purpose, such as PowerPoint or Google Slides. You may cut and paste text from a word-processing application and may want to use other programs like Photoshop or iMovie to edit images or video to embed in your slides.

- For the handout component, how will you design it so that the message and tone are consistent with your rhetorical situation and the content of your presentation? Would a hand-drawn representation of your content be appropriate for your audience and purpose? Should you use a word processor to create a straightforward and polished text-only document, or could an infographic, made with a site like Canva, help you to create a more condensed and engaging communication?

The best way to make a decision about whether you should create an analog or digital project is to keep in mind your audience and purpose while also thinking about your access to and ability with various technologies.

Assessing Technological Affordances

Choosing a technology for your project will depend on many factors, including your project's rhetorical situation, the modes and media you need to suit that situation, and the affordances of the technologies available to you to design with those rhetorical needs in mind. When choosing a technology, take time to explore what is available to you, what you know how to do, and what skills you can learn or software you can acquire given your budget and project timeline.

The list that follows identifies technologies that can be used to create or edit different media. Some are free, some are not, and some have trial versions you can explore. The list includes some of the most commonly used applications, but plenty of other software is available, and more is developed all the time. (This list may become outdated, as technologies change rapidly, but searching for some of these programs might help you find other, more up-to-date ones.) Additionally, since mobile devices and tablets have begun offering more robust media capturing and editing capabilities, there is a large and ever-growing selection of mobile multimodal authoring/editing apps. A quick brainstorm with your project team or classmates will produce a robust list for each mobile platform type.

Some of these programs have affordances that allow you to produce multiple kinds of media objects, so our list based on media type and genre is fluid. For instance, if you're working on a storytelling project, you might find useful tools in the interactive stories and games section, augmented/virtual reality section, mapping section, and others! And you might build part of a project in a tool from one category (a timeline) to put into a tool within another category (video or website, or both) to reach your audience. We've focused on

Technology Choices for Multimodal Authoring

I need to design/find . . .	I can use . . .
Animation	Blender, Comic Life, Adobe Animate, Synfig, Adobe After Effects, Xtranormal, Adobe Photoshop, OpenToonz, Animation Paper
Audio	Audacity, GarageBand, Twisted Wave, WavePad, Logic Pro, Pro Tools, Adobe Audition, Audio Ocean, SoundCloud, Reaper, Studio One, FL Studio, SoundCite
Augmented/Virtual Reality	KnightLab's Scene, Adobe Aero
Captioning	Otter Speech to Text, YouTube, MovieCaptioner, SubtitleEdit, Aegisub
Color Palettes	Coolors, Dribble, Mycolor.space, Adobe Color
Images	GIMP, Adobe Photoshop, Adobe Illustrator, Adobe Spark Post, CorelDRAW, Microsoft Paint, Canva, Fotor, Pixlr Editor, Paint.NET, Affinity Publisher, Photo, Designer, Capture One, Adobe Dimension
Infographics and Data Visualization	Piktochart, Venngage, Visme, Easel.ly, Canva, PowerPoint, Adobe Illustrator, Tableau, Microsoft Excel
Interactive Stories & Games	Twine, Lightwell, KnightLab's Timeline.js, Scratch, Unity, ClickTeam Fusion, RPG Maker
Maps/Cartography	Google My Maps, ArcGIS StoryMaps, KnightLab's StoryMap
Micro- and Multimedia Blogs	Blogger, WordPress, Weebly, Moveable Type, TypePad, Tumblr, Medium, Twitter, Pinterest, Flipgrip, TikTok, Wakelet, Sutori, Flipgrid
Mobile Writing/Designing	TikTok, Instagram, Snapseed, Apple Clips, Voiceflow
Presentation/Slide Show	Microsoft PowerPoint, Apple Keynote, Prezi, Google Slides, Microsoft Sway, Adobe Spark Page
Print-Like Publications/Posters	Microsoft Publisher, Adobe InDesign, Affinity Publisher, Adobe Acrobat Pro, Pressbooks, Canva, PowerPoint, Scribus, iBooks
Screen Captures	Snapz Pro X, Camtasia, Snagit, Screencast-O-Matic, Jing, QuickTime, Microsoft Stream, TinyTake, Kaltura Capture, Nimbus
Stock Assets	Creative Commons, Wikimedia Commons, Pixabay, Unsplash, Pexels, Google Fonts, Font Squirrel, 1001 Free Fonts, YouTube Studio Audio Library, Soundbible

Technology Choices for Multimodal Authoring (*continued*)

I need to design/find . . .	I can use . . .
Video	Apple iMovie, Final Cut Pro, Media Composer, Adobe Premiere Pro, YouTube Editor, Camtasia, Adobe Spark, Microsoft Photos, VidGrid Screen Recorder, Adobe Premiere Rush, Shotcut, Adobe After Effects
Video Streaming	Twitch, Ecamm, StreamYard, Microsoft Stream, Wirecast Studio, PlaceIt, ActivePresenter
Website/User Interface/ User Experience	Adobe Dreamweaver, Adobe Spark, KompoZer, Nvu, Squarespace, Wix, Scalar, Weebly, Google Sites, Divi, Elementor, GitHub Pages, Adobe XD, and text editors such as BBEdit, TextWrangler, NotePad, and Atom

digital tools in this list, but of course you can also use construction paper, stencils, printers, scissors, rulers, and so on. The Touchpoint at the end of this section, Conducting a Technology Review (pp. 177–78), asks you to research what some of those affordances are in relation to your project. In the meantime, consider the following example of one student's research process to assess which technologies she would use in her project.

In one of Kristin's classes, students were asked to create multimodal deliverables for an imaginary election campaign of their choosing. One student, Oliviah, created a fictional candidate for president, Olive Jenkins. Oliviah thought the best three deliverables to make would be a door hanger, a poster (see **Fig. 7.3**), and a website (see **Fig. 7.4**). As she later reflected in a writer/designer justification statement describing the project, "I chose these because the website appeals to those who use the internet to find information about political candidates, the door hanger is a good way to get the attention of the people on a more personal level, and the poster

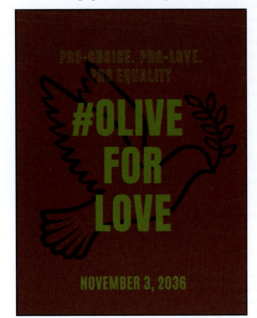

Figure 7.3 Oliviah's Poster for Her Fictional Presidential Candidate, Olive Jenkins

Oliviah first designed her poster in order to clarify for herself the overall design concept she wanted to use in this campaign. She chose an image of a dove (a symbol of peace) as well as earth tones, as she felt it helped avoid any strong partisan preconceived notions.

Courtesy of Oliviah Brown

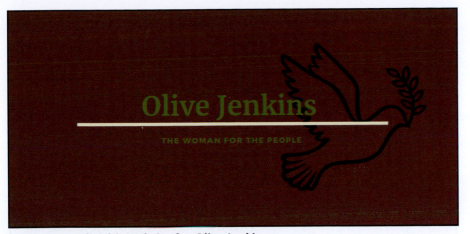

Figure 7.4 Oliviah's Website for Olive Jenkins

Oliviah mimicked the poster design when creating her website.

Courtesy of Oliviah Brown

because it provides the primary logo and concept for my candidate and can be adapted into different media such as billboards, social media advertisements, and other physical deliverables."

In the past, Oliviah had used Canva for designing things like posters, but she had not made a website before. Kristin's class did not directly teach any web development, so Oliviah had to think carefully about what would work best given her project goals, her timeline, and her learning style. Oliviah knew she wanted to create a very simple website that highlighted Olive Jenkins's biography, beliefs, and platform. She also knew that her timeline was short, and that making a poster and door hanger along with the website was going to leave her little time to learn a new software program like WordPress. After doing some exploring on the Canva website, she learned she could use it to make a simple one-page website.

Touchpoint: Conducting a Technology Review

Review the Technology Choices for Multimodal Authoring chart on pages 175–76 and choose a set of programs that you think might be the best match for your project's needs. (Depending on your project, you may need several different kinds of programs, such as a photo editor, an audio editor, and a Web editor.) If you are not currently at work on a multimodal project, use this exercise to explore a program you're curious about or would like to use in a future project. If you are writing an essay, use this exercise to practice thinking about technological affordances in programs such as Microsoft Word.

Create a chart for each technology or program you want to explore. In the left column of each chart, list the questions below.

- What does this tool do? What is its purpose? (Is it an HTML editor, a sound editor, a social media application, or something else?) What kinds of texts are usually made using this technology?

- Is the tool platform-specific (Mac/PC/Linux), or is it available only online?

- Do you have access to this software? Do you already own a copy, is it installed on computers in labs you have access to, or is it available as a free download or on a trial basis for a long-enough period of time for you to complete your project?

- How does the program work? (This is not meant to be a huge tutorial; just note the basic compositional or editorial features.)

- How steep is the learning curve, and will you have the time and resources to learn enough about the technology to complete your project? What are some tutorial sites or videos that seem effective for learning the basics?

- What do you need to do before you can start designing in the technology? (Do you collect assets elsewhere and import them into the program, or do you "record" directly into it?) Do you need additional technologies, like an external video camera or audio recorder, to make this tool function the way it's supposed to?

- What are the benefits of using this particular technology for the genre of your multimodal project? What are the drawbacks? What does the technology do or not do that will affect how you compose a text in your chosen genre? What file formats does it import and export?

As you research a particular technology, jot down your answer to each question in the right column of the corresponding chart. Compare your answers about the different technologies to help you choose the technology that will best suit your needs. If none are suitable, pick another subset of programs and begin your research process again. Then, based on the affordances you've listed in your chart, choose which program (or set) you will explore further to complete your multimodal project.

Drafting Your Project: Static, Dynamic, and Timeline-Based Texts

As we've discussed throughout *Writer/Designer*, your rhetorical situation shapes your project and the variety of forms it might take. Not only will each final product look different and be used in different ways, but the form and function of each draft will also differ. For example, if you are creating a *static* text like a poster or a flyer, your drafting process might produce some quick sketches, followed by more detailed mock-ups of design plans, and conclude with a polished version printed on glossy paper. In contrast, if you are planning a *dynamic* website for your project, you might begin with some notes on what elements you want the interface to include, followed by a paper-based sketch of the site's layout and navigation, followed by a wireframe to specify the visual details like width and image placement. The drafting process might then culminate in a rough but functional version of your site that you can use to get feedback from your audience and to test for usability. (You can learn more about all of these types of drafts later in this section.)

No matter what mode you are working in or what kind of draft you create, these initial versions of a text allow writer/designers to work through some of the trickier aspects of a project for themselves, as well as to show more concrete drafts to audiences or stakeholders for feedback. In this chapter, we highlight the drafting process and products for three different categories of texts you might produce.

Static texts are those that are set or fixed once an author has completed the writing/designing process. For example, once you finish a written essay or a printed menu, the content itself doesn't change when the audience interacts with it. They simply read through it in a linear way. Drafts for static texts include rapid prototypes, outlines, models, and some mock-ups. In contrast, **dynamic interactive texts** are those where the audience has choices about which parts of the content they read or interact with at any given time, and the text doesn't advance without the ongoing choices of the reader. The best example is a website where users choose the order of the text based on the links they select. As a writer/designer, you have to consider not only your overall message but also how the parts will fit together when read in any order. Drafts for dynamic interactive texts include wireframes and mock-ups. Finally, a **timeline-based text** is one the audience experiences in a linear sequence, such as a film, video, or podcast. As the author, you arrange segments of content (audio, video, written text, etc.) to lead your audience along a path, building your message or argument with each element you weave in. Drafts for timeline-based texts include storyboards, scripts, and rough cuts.

While all drafts are used to bring ideas to life in a physical form, each draft also takes a form that is appropriate to the genre in which you are working. Some of the drafting activities in the following sections can apply across this spectrum of text types, while others, like storyboards, are appropriate for only certain kinds of texts. In this chapter we discuss these drafting activities in relation to the kinds of texts that generally use them. But keep in mind, you can adapt these draft stages or combine them in ways that best fit the medium or genre you are creating.

Prototyping for Static Texts

Product designers create drafts of their static projects that are sometimes called **prototypes** (see **Fig. 7.5**). The term *prototype* can be used broadly to mean "draft" in a variety of forms, but it is often used to refer to a draft that is functional or visual enough to present to reviewers or stakeholders, giving them a clear idea of how the final project will work or look. Prototypes also allow writer/designers to see what their project would look like in a physical form before it is complete so that it can be tested.

To avoid spending time, money, and energy on final products that don't work, designers often use a process called *rapid prototyping*. Tom Kelly, creative director at the design consultancy company IDEO, is well known for developing his company's motto: "fail often, succeed sooner." This mantra, now widely adopted in all kinds of business and industry, encourages quick and continual refinement of new ideas based on analysis of what did and didn't work in previous versions. That is, rather than spending weeks, months, or even years perfecting a design that may then soon be obsolete or otherwise doesn't work, rapid prototyping encourages writer/designers to draft and test small changes on a fast and perpetual basis. This has the advantages of shorter development times; creating features that are more fitting for target audiences; and, ultimately, designing texts that successfully fit the rhetorical

Figure 7.5 **Rapid Prototyping in Action with a 3D Printer**

The printer adds gingerbread to this model of a medieval church.

Courtesy of William Kempton

situation. Rapid prototypes are becoming increasingly common as the availability of 3D printers becomes more widespread (check with your campus library, instructional technology center, or entrepreneurship organization to see if there is one you can use locally).

While 3D printer models are often associated with rapid prototyping processes, there are many other draft types that would also work during this stage of the design process. Draft types for static multimodal projects, such as outlines, sketches, and models, can all be used to solicit quick and repeated feedback from users and to make design changes as a result.

Outlines

One of the easiest ways to get started drafting any kind of project is to make an **outline**, which lists main points, followed by supporting points and evidence. Outlines may be formal, using roman numerals and letters to designate hierarchies (I, ii, A, b), or they may be simplified, using indents and bullets. By starting to map out the general organization and structure of your plan, you can begin to visualize what kinds of assets you'll need to gather (textual research, images, video clips, etc.) and how you can arrange them to lead your audience through your argument or message.

In **Figure 7.6**, one student created a basic outline to plan the content and structure of their project, which analyzed how sororities at the student's university construct their identities through the photos they post to Instagram. One of the student's points focused on sisterhood and how pictures of sorority sisters holding hands help shape this identity. The outline helped the student organize their ideas, so when they wrote their final essay, they integrated images from various sorority Instagram feeds as visual evidence for their analysis, including pictures of sisters holding hands, which you can see in **Figure 7.7**. While the final essay's organization changed a little from the student's original outline, starting with that drafting document laid out a clear map for the student to approach the writing/designing of their project.

Sketches

One of the best ways to begin transforming your static project ideas into concrete designs is to sketch them on paper. Almost any type of text can benefit from producing **sketches**, and sketching your initial ideas has a number of advantages. First, you can quickly generate a number of options without having to wrangle

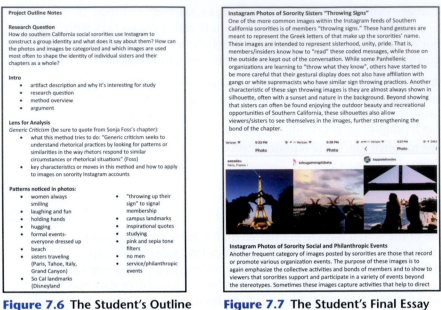

Project Outline Notes

Research Question
How do southern California social sororities use Instagram to construct a group identity and what does it say about them? How can the photos and images be categorized and which images are used most often to shape the identity of individual sisters and their chapters as a whole?

Intro
- artifact description and why it's interesting for study
- research question
- method overview
- argument

Lens for Analysis
Generic Criticism (be sure to quote from Sonja Foss's chapter):
- what this method tries to do: "Generic criticism seeks to understand rhetorical practices by looking for patterns or similarities in the way rhetors respond to similar circumstances or rhetorical situations" (Foss)
- key characteristics or moves in this method and how to apply to images on sorority Instagram accounts

Patterns noticed in photos:
- women always smiling
- laughing and fun
- holding hands
- hugging
- formal events-everyone dressed up
- beach
- sisters traveling (Paris, Tahoe, Italy, Grand Canyon)
- So Cal landmarks (Disneyland

- "throwing up their sign" to signal membership
- campus landmarks
- inspirational quotes
- studying
- pink and sepia tone filters
- no men
- service/philanthropic events

Figure 7.6 The Student's Outline
Courtesy of Jennifer Sheppard

Instagram Photos of Sorority Sisters "Throwing Signs"
One of the more common images within the Instagram feeds of Southern California sororities is of members "throwing signs." These hand gestures are meant to represent the Greek letters of that make up the sororities' name. These images are intended to represent sisterhood, unity, pride. That is, members/insiders know how to "read" these coded messages, while those on the outside are kept out of the conversation. While some Panhellenic organizations are learning to "throw what they know," others have started to be more careful that their gestural display does not also have affiliation with gangs or white supremacists who have similar sign throwing practices. Another characteristic of these sign throwing images is they are almost always shown in silhouette, often with a sunset and nature in the background. Beyond showing that sisters can often be found enjoying the outdoor beauty and recreational opportunities of Southern California, these silhouettes also allow viewers/sisters to see themselves in the images, further strengthening the bond of the chapter.

Instagram Photos of Sorority Social and Philanthropic Events
Another frequent category of images posted by sororities are those that record or promote various organization events. The purpose of these images is to again emphasize the collective activities and bonds of members and to show to viewers that sororities support and participate in a variety of events beyond the stereotypes. Sometimes these images capture activities that help to direct

Figure 7.7 The Student's Final Essay
Courtesy of Jennifer Sheppard

with software. Second, because you have spent little time on these sketches, you are likely to be more receptive to tweaks or major overhauls based on feedback from peers or stakeholders. In the sample sketch (**Fig. 7.8**) and revised mock-up (**Fig. 7.9**), several small but important refinements, such as dropping the second row of horizontal navigation and incorporating the orange color, resulted from suggestions during a peer review session of the initial sketch. Remember, making beautiful sketches is not the point, so don't worry if you don't have the skills of an artist. You are trying

Figure 7.8 Sample Sketch
Courtesy of Hannah Willis

Figure 7.9 Revised Mock-Up
Courtesy of Hannah Willis

to visualize your possibilities here and to work out some initial challenges before you spend too much time going down a path that dead-ends.

Models

Models are drafts for static, analog texts, and they help writer/ designers see what their project would look like in physical form, often in miniature, before it is completed. Models are important because they offer a concrete representation of a project so that design and development plans can be reviewed and revised *before* major time and resources are invested.

Everyday products we use, from cups to buildings, are all types of multimodal texts that start their compositional life as sketches and then models. Models come in a range of completeness and are often useful and valuable products in their own right—especially as objects to provide reflection and revision opportunities with stakeholders who may not be able to envision your 3D work in a 2D sketch.

The Skissernas (or Sketches) Museum in Lund, Sweden, is dedicated to showing the artistic process of public art by exhibiting only the sketches, models, and early paintings of artists whose work appears in final form at other venues. In this photo of one of the main galleries, visitors can see the in-progress artwork on display literally from floor to ceiling, as well as in filing cabinets they can open that are positioned against the walls.

Figure 7.10 **A Museum Dedicated to Multimodal Models**

Photo: Åke E:son Lindman, courtesy of Skissernas Museum

⊙— Touchpoint: Sketching a Draft

Begin an outline, rough sketch, or model of what your current project might look like. Or, if you're not currently working on a project, do some initial sketches for an invitation you might design for your next party or event. Don't worry if your drawing skills aren't sophisticated. The point here is to generate ideas quickly and explore possibilities about which elements to include and how to arrange them, not to create a final product.

1. Refer back to your rhetorical situation and make a list of the most import-ant features you need to include. Keep in mind that while your design is important in setting your project's tone and helping your readers navigate through it, your most important task is to communicate your message.

2. Once you have a rough sketch you are satisfied with, create two or three more, trying to make them as different as possible from the first. Many designers refer to these small, quick sketches as **thumbnails**, and they use them to rough out their initial ideas.

By forcing yourself to come up with several different approaches, you'll work through the pros and cons of several possibilities and may find, in later iterations, that combining elements from different designs best meets your needs.

Designing Drafts of Dynamic Texts

Creating drafts of dynamic texts, such as websites and pop-up books, requires that you attend to a project's navigational features. You might use static drafting techniques like outlining and sketch-ing to get you part of the way in your design, but dynamic drafting techniques like making wireframes and mock-ups allow you to really map out the action of your interactive project.

Wireframes

Wireframes are used for dynamic, interactive texts in that they are created to be blueprints or skeletal outlines for how a project will be organized. They are most often used in planning websites: in addi-tion to arranging content, they also specify important components of the site's interface and navigation and how those will look and function across each page within the site.

In **Figure 7.11**, the designer of a website for family nutrition has spec-ified the placement of several elements on the page: navigation cues

Figure 7.11 A Wireframe for a Website

Courtesy Edreanne Calaycay

and icons, sections for specific audiences such as parents and children, and footer content that will be available on every page. Wireframes are an important part of the development process for websites because they offer a quick way to assess usability and how the layout of a site can support or hinder users' access to information.

You can use online tools that were created for speed sketching of interface layouts, such as Balsamiq, which features pre-made navigation icons and templates that can be dragged and dropped with ease, allowing writer/designers to map layout ideas quickly without worrying too much about aesthetics or the coding necessary to create a website.

Mock-Ups

A **mock-up** is a rough layout of a screen or page (see **Fig. 7.12**). Mock-ups differ from sketches (see pp. 181–82) because they are typically used further along in the development process, after you have decided on which sketched idea you want to pursue. They are commonly used for drafting any type of static composition that is primarily visual, such as a poster, an album cover, or a brochure. They are also used frequently in the design of dynamic, interactive texts like websites because they provide a visual snapshot of a site's basic layout and design.

Essentially, a mock-up is a visual outline of a project. A good mock-up should include the proposed layout, colors, images, fonts, and recurring elements such as headers. Though mock-ups may include the actual textual content, often they do not. The idea is to create

Figure 7.12 Tapiola Veterinary Hospital Website Mock-Up

This mock-up, designed in PowerPoint, shows where the main content on each page of this site will be as well as how the navigation will work within the drop-down menus.

Courtesy of Kristin Arola

Figure 7.13 A Mock-Up Design for The Kitchen Sync

Courtesy of Nick Winters

a kind of road map that shows where everything will eventually go, not to actually create the finished product. Web authors often compose mock-ups by hand, on paper, or in some type of screen-based software such as Photoshop. You can also create mock-ups using word processors, spreadsheets, or slideshow software. It's not so much *how* you create the mock-up that's important as *what* the mock-up illustrates.

Figure 7.13 shows a professional Web design mock-up for The Kitchen Sync, a boutique kitchen supply store located in Wenatchee, Washington. The clients (the owners of the store) wanted a website that provided a professional boutique feel while also showcasing the different products the store had to offer. The main goal was to get people to visit the physical store itself. While the clients had some ideas about what they wanted the site to look like, the Web designer wanted to show them a rough layout with a few different color and image options. Notice that on the left-hand side of this mock-up you see possible colors, textures, and images. On the right-hand side, you see possible headings and buttons.

As writer/designers, we often find that our first ideas about how to arrange elements need tweaking once we start visualizing them on paper, and they sometimes don't work at all. By first sketching out really rough layouts or wireframes and then revising and making changes in our mock-ups, we ultimately save ourselves time and create more successful designs.

◉— Touchpoint: Drafting Your Wireframe and Mock-Up

If you are designing a wireframe or mock-up for your multimodal project—or if you are a classmate or stakeholder reviewing another writer/designer's draft—use the following checklist to consider questions or evaluate the design.

❑ Is the proposed layout evident? Is it consistent across all possible iterations (pages) of the text? If the layout needs to change to indicate different sections or areas of a text, are those variations indicated in separate or supplementary mock-ups?

❑ Is the color scheme clearly indicated? Is it appropriate for the rhetorical situation and for readability?

❑ If images are used, is their relative placement on the page or screen mock-up purposeful and consistent across all versions?

❑ Are example fonts provided, and if so, do they adequately reflect the rhetorical needs of the text? For example, did you use display type for headlines and body type for larger amounts of written content?

❑ Are the navigational elements shown or indicated? Are they clear for users? Are they consistent across all iterations?

Composing Timeline-Based Drafts

Timeline-based drafts are used for any type of project that includes a chronological progression that audiences will watch, read, or hear. If you are creating a video, audio text, or a timed slideshow, for example, the drafting methods we discuss in this section—storyboards, scripts, and rough cuts—might be what you need.

Storyboards

A **storyboard**, as seen in **Figures 7.14–7.17**, is a sequence of drawings, much like a comic book or visual outline, that represents the movement, spatial arrangement, and soundtracks of objects or characters in shots, screens, or scenes. Because they illustrate elements in a sequence, storyboards work best for timeline-based projects, such as videos, audio pieces, or animations.

A storyboard represents a text that moves through time, such as a video, visual podcast, or an animation. Like mock-ups, storyboards may include rough visuals, but they use visuals to show the sequence of the project as well as written descriptions of the actions or sound effects that need to take place at each moment. Storyboards can be incredibly complex, but a simple storyboard consisting only of stick figures and a few arrows to show directionality can also be surprisingly effective. As with mock-ups, the important thing is not how artistic the storyboards are but that they indicate what elements (setting, script, images, soundtrack, or effects) and actions (movement, lighting, camera angle, etc.) need to occur at which point.

The goal of an effective storyboard, no matter its level of complexity, is to capture as much information as possible and help you decide what shots you'll need to film, what audio you'll need to record, or what images you'll need to capture *before* the filming, recording, or animating begins. (See Chapter 6 for more on collecting and organizing assets.) Good planning now will save you lots of time and frustration later on, so it's worth the effort. Similar to a

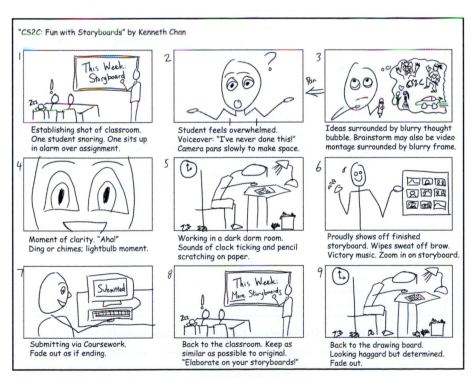

Figure 7.14 A Storyboard about Making Storyboards

Courtesy of Kenneth Chan

mock-up, a storyboard can also help you get feedback on your basic design so that you can adjust it if it isn't working for your audience.

When creating your storyboard, you'll want to think about including notes on the following elements:

- Setting
- Movement by characters or objects

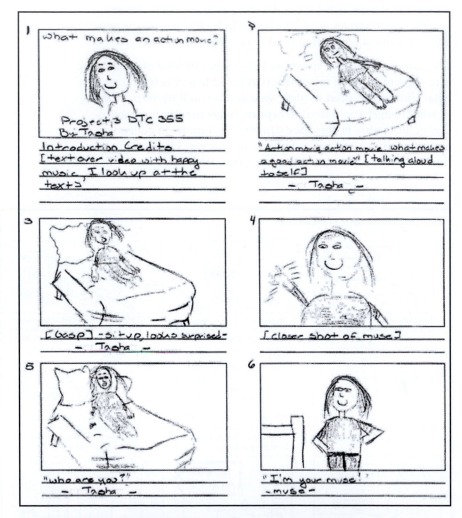

Figure 7.15 The First Six Panels of Courteney's Storyboard

These panels show her introduction of the topic (Panel 1), the beginning of her narrative-based analysis (Panels 2–3, in Courteney's bedroom), and the main characters in the analysis (Panels 4–6, Courteney and her "muse").

Courtesy of Courteney Dowd

- Script/dialogue
- Soundtrack or sound effects
- Shooting angle

Of course, depending on the genre of your project, you may want to make notes on other elements as well.

For instance, Courteney was creating a three-minute video-based analysis on effective action films and had sixty-four panels in her storyboard. **Figure 7.15** (p. 190) is a small segment of Courteney's entire storyboard. You can see that you don't need to be an amazing artist to compose an effective storyboard; you just need to include enough detail so that your audience, teammates, or instructor can figure out what you intend to do and give you feedback on it, and so that you have an outline to work with once you start capturing content.

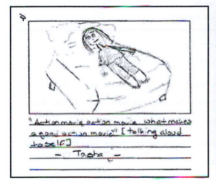

Figure 7.16 Courteney's Drawing of Herself in Bed (Panel 2 of 64)
Courtesy of Courteney Dowd

Figure 7.17 Courteney's Video of That Scene
Courtesy of Courteney Dowd

Scripts

If your multimodal project will include audio or video, you may need to create a **script**. A script is a draft for a timeline-based project that allows you to specify linguistic content (what will actually get said or shown) and other multimodal elements such as sound effects, visual effects or transitions, stage directions, and more. If you've created a storyboard for your project, writing a script is the next step in putting those ideas into action. As shown in **Figure 7.18**, a script typically includes dialogue, with clear identification of who will say what and when. It will also include details about *how* that content will be presented, such as sound effects, lighting, or the tone of an actor/ narrator, and will place them within a timeline to see how all the pieces fit together. A script for a video project will likely include even more detail about what visuals will appear on screen and how they will align with other multimodal content, like music or dialogue.

Writing a script in advance of recording—even if there is no voice-over or dialogue—is useful for accessibility purposes. You can turn your draft script into a transcript to upload with the media files you prepare. That way, readers with different vision, hearing, or neurological accessibility levels can still engage with your project. Plus, making your project accessible to all users is the law in many countries and when creating content for government agencies.

Your script is a detailed road map for turning your storyboards into a working project, but keep in mind that you'll likely have to make adjustments as you begin filming/recording.

Figure 7.18 A Script for a Radio Commercial

Courtesy of Kristin Arola

Client: Whitman County
Job Title: 30sec Radio Commercial
Commercial Title: Your Opinion Matters!

MUSIC: (INSTUMENTAL OF THE STAR SPANGLED BANNER)

WOMAN: (FRUSTRATED) Are you tired of all the promises our community makes towards making our community better and safer, but in the end they just never get around to actually fulfilling these promises?

MAN: (ANGRY) Yes, but I wish that during the GOP meeting my opinion would actually be heard on the matter!

WOMAN: (CURIOUS) Well have you ever actually attended a GOP meeting in Whitman County?

MAN: (ASHAMED) Well... No

WOMAN: (EAGER) You should! If you were to attend the next Whitman County GOP meeting, then your opinion would be heard and we could put an end to all of these empty promises. Plus, I heard there is free pizza at every meeting!

MUSIC: (INSTUMENTAL OF THE STAR SPANGLED BANNER OUT)

Rough Cuts

Rough cuts (like **Fig. 7.19**) are another step in composing time-line-based projects. Using all of the work you've done in previous parts of the drafting process (sketches, storyboards, wireframes),

Figure 7.19 A Sample Rough Cut

This rough cut of a video bonnie lenore kyburz is making has all the static photos and animated screen captures in their correct place in the video project timeline (see the bottom half). The sources are also included in the upper left-hand corner. She also still needs to add titles and some transitions between the visuals, but this version of the video is appropriate for a rough cut review, which viewers can watch in the preview window (in the upper right-hand corner).

Courtesy of bonnie lenore kyburz

rough cuts are your first attempts at actually building your project and putting the pieces into sequence. Rough cuts are usually missing significant elements such as background soundtracks (with audio or video projects), titles and transitions (audio and video projects), navigation (websites), permanent graphics (posters), and so on.

In addition, rough cuts shouldn't include tightly edited assets, because feedback on your rough cut might indicate that you need to revise your project in a different direction. If you've cut your video down to a ten-second clip, and then reviewers tell you they'd like to see a little more of it, you're out of luck. You want to have enough content left in your assets to be able to add different shots or material to your revised project if your reviewers suggest such changes.

◎— **Touchpoint: Drafting Your Storyboard**

For most timeline-based texts, a storyboard will be necessary. If you are designing a timeline-based text for your multimodal project—or if you are a classmate or stakeholder reviewing another writer/designer's draft—use the following checklist to consider questions or evaluate the design.

❏ Is the initial setting or context clearly evident? How is each setting or segment change represented auditorially, visually, spatially, or linguistically—via titles, transitions, or other means?

❏ Is each character/interview/subject matter differentiated in some way (if it's necessary to do so)?

❏ Are important character or object movements indicated? (For example, if it's important that a character is seen rolling his or her eyes, have you used arrows around the eyeballs or something else to indicate that movement? Or if a car is supposed to exit the right side of the frame, how have you shown that?)

❏ Are snippets of major dialogue included underneath the storyboard visuals? If not, what are the key ideas that need to be expressed in each scene or segment?

❏ Are sound effects or musical scores noted (usually under the dialogue or scene)? Do you indicate what these audio elements will be and how long or loud they will be?

Getting Feedback on Your Rough Drafts

After you have a draft completed, it's a good time to invoke the feedback loop, particularly from your peers. We discuss peer review in more detail in Chapter 5 in reference to your final drafts (see Peer Reviewing Multimodal Projects, pp. 121–24), but before you get that far, you might also want to present your mock-up, wireframe, storyboard, or rough cut to your instructor or other stakeholders. The presentation of this rough draft may be formal (presenting to a client) or informal (conferencing with a teacher or workshopping with classmates), depending on your writing situation.

Here are some tips for presenting your in-progress rough draft to stakeholders:

- Be able to say why you've made your design choices—for example, you might explain that you chose the color scheme and navigation system for your website mock-up to match the interests of the site's intended audience, or that the nontraditional sequence of your storyboard's scenes is crucial to your text's purpose. At the same time, be open to the comments and suggestions of those you share these early designs with. Sometimes writer/designers get so immersed in their work that they lose a bit of perspective. Keep in mind that feedback from others can help you improve and build on your ideas by tailoring them to the needs of the stakeholders and the rhetorical situation.

- Prepare a list of questions you'd like to ask your reviewers. Refer to checklists in *Writer/Designer* like the Mock-Ups and Storyboards sections (pp. 186–89) to determine the areas that you might want your reviewers to focus on. If you're submitting a rough cut, ask your reviewers to make sure nothing sticks out as odd, out of place, inaudible, or nonsensical. Remember, this is just a rough version of your project. The roughly edited assets should tell enough of the story or argument for your feedback loop to catch what (if anything) doesn't belong and what still may need to be added. (Refer back to Chapter 5, Putting Together a Complete Draft for Your Primary Audience on pp. 117–20, for more on the feedback loop and peer review.)

- Research the genre requirements for your project and provide reviewers with a genre checklist (if appropriate) as they review your documents. (Refer back to Chapter 3 for more on genre.)

- If your stakeholders or colleagues offer feedback, assess that feedback for its usefulness in relation to your project's rhetorical situation, and revise your draft accordingly. (Refer back to Chapter 5, Revising Your Multimodal Project on pp. 130–33, for more on revision plans.)

Preserving Your Assets with Metadata

Deciding on a delivery medium and drafting your multimodal project fulfills only part of the requirements for finalizing all of your hard work. Let's say your delivery medium is the Web, or more specifically a third-party hosting site such as YouTube, Instagram, Wix, or Wikimedia. You could just upload your project and walk away. (Although you should tell your client where your project is located!) Maybe you've created a radio essay that you will turn in for

Figure 7.20 StoryCorps Web Page with Metadata

The Web page for this Studs Terkel story contains metadata in the form of a title, a recording location, credits, a description, and other data.

a class project, but you also will upload it to a radio-essay website such as StoryCorps (as seen in **Fig. 7.20**). How will your intended audience actually *find* your project? How will other people know what it is? How will a computer, which can only scan text, search for your audio file? Metadata is the answer. **Metadata** is data about data: information about a piece of content that can tell a reader who created the content, what it represents, when it was recorded, and other bits of information that make your project findable and usable by others.

You've probably seen keywords, tags, categories, and other meta-data on media-sharing sites like Wikimedia Commons. Each media element that an author uploads to Wikimedia Commons has to include written information or data *about* the media element so that Wikimedia can help other users find that element. Without this metadata, the media element won't be easily found by, say, a user searching for the perfect audio sound effect of rain falling in Glenshaw, Pennsylvania, to include in her documentary about that tiny town.

A screenshot of the summary section of the Wikimedia Commons page for the sound effect of "Heavy rain in Glenshaw, PA" (**Fig. 7.21**) shows some of the metadata for this one file. The metadata includes a description of the sound effect, the date it was recorded, the source of the work, the author who created it, what the file's permissions are, where the file was recorded, and a bunch of other information further down the page. Researchers can search for the town name (if they need a specific geographic location), date (if they need a specific time period), and so on from either a search engine or from the Wikimedia Commons home page, where users can browse for content by topic, media type, author, copyright license, or publication source (among other options). All of this information is metadata that the file's author included when they uploaded the file to the Web. Additionally, supporting written material such as transcripts of audio/video files and descriptions from proposals can function as metadata for your final project. Including all of this information will help make sure that your project is sustainable.

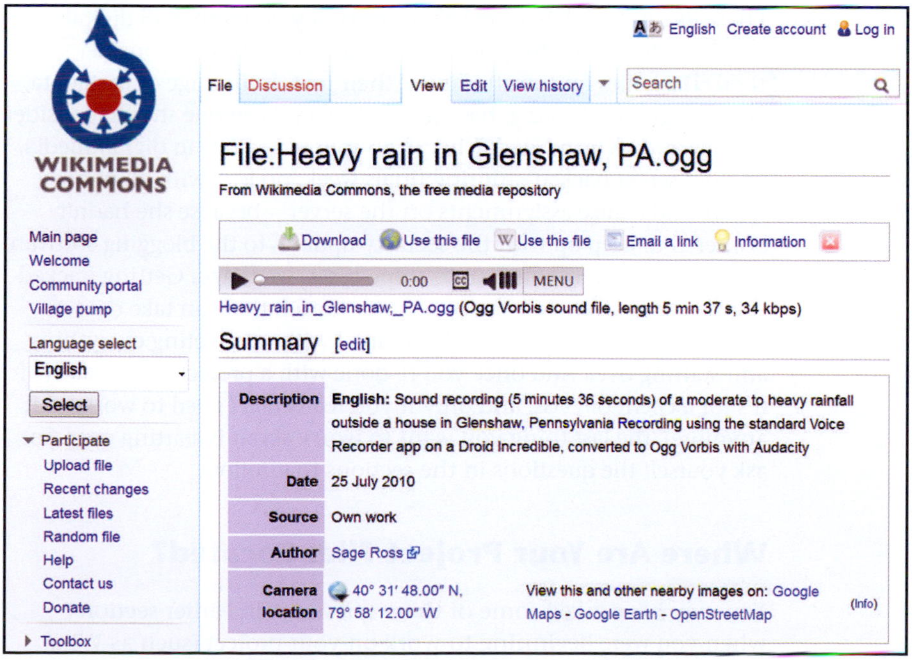

Figure 7.21 Finding Metadata on a Wikimedia Commons Page

Preparing for the Multimodal Afterlife

Once you've finished your multimodal project, consider what will happen once you walk away from it. Unless you've set up a *Mission: Impossible*–style self-destruct option (warn your clients if you do), your text will continue to have a life of its own long after you've forgotten about it. This can be good, bad, or worse.

- **Good:** Maybe the TikTok you posted of you and your cat doing a version of Dogg Face's Morning Vibe skateboard, juice, and Fleetwood Mac's "Dreams" goes viral and you and your cat get invited to appear on a late-night TV show.

- **Bad:** The TikTok sent people to your account, which also includes a TikTok of you smoking and dancing inappropriately at a New Year's Eve party, and is seen by the human resources department for a company where you recently interviewed for a job that you really need. And they don't hire you.

- **Worse:** You already work for the company, and they fire you because somebody in the background of one of one of your TikToks was doing something not just stupid or silly but illegal, and you're now a party to that illegality.

These examples relate primarily to **privacy** issues that all digital media authors need to consider, but authors must also consider **security** issues for the afterlife of their text. In this age of metadata, face-recognition tagging, hackers, and spam, everyone should consider privacy and security. Even Cheryl, a supposed expert in digital media, had her server hacked—during finals week, no less, with all of her syllabi and course assignments on the server—because she hadn't bothered to keep up with the security updates to the blogging software she had installed months or, in some cases, years ago. Getting hacked is just one example of a major security breach that can take days or weeks to fix, if it can even be fixed at all without deleting everything and starting over. And once you're done with a project (particularly if it's for a client or class, and only if you really *don't* need to work on it anymore), the last thing you want to worry about is starting over. So ask yourself the questions in the sections that follow.

Where Are Your Project Files Located?

You may have asked some of these questions in earlier sections when you were beginning to work on your project (such as What Does Your Audience Need?, pp. 171–74), but it's important to refer to this list of questions at multiple points during the write/design process and after your work is completed to ensure privacy, security, and stability for your project.

- If they're stored online, is that online location private (password-protected and/or available only to a limited group of collaborators or clients)?
  - Who do you want to continue having access to that private location? Remove/unshare/delete any users that should no longer have access.
  - Is the location secure enough to leave the files there as a backup?
  - What will you do if that backup location stops providing the service you're using? How often will you check back to see whether the service may be discontinued? Can you set up an automatic notification?
- Is that online location public (available on the Web for any search engine to scan or a potential boss to see)?
  - Do you need to have that final draft available publicly? If not, pull it down. If you do, perhaps you're not really done with this project, and you need to make plans (regarding financial or labor resources, time management, and other things outside the scope of this book's discussion) for maintaining it.
  - Does the metadata for the project allow a level of privacy that you're comfortable with now and will be comfortable with into the future? Will you be able to update the metadata to reflect your changing privacy needs as you get older?

How Long Are You Responsible for the Project?

- How often do you need to check in to that location to make sure your privacy is being maintained?
- How often do you need to perform any upgrades or updates to the location to ensure

Figure 7.22 Where Is Your Media Archived?

Don't rely on social media platforms to keep your valuable media content safe. These Facebook photos posted in 2012 are now impossible to find. Always keep backups.

Cheryl Ball and Xuxa Rodriguez

your privacy and security? Can you set up an automatic update or arrange to be notified automatically when updates need to be made?

- Should you copy online files (whether public or private) to an offline location and delete the online versions?

- Do you need to keep a copy of the files at all?

- If so, what kind of storage device will you keep them on, and how will you ensure that you will be able to use that storage device five years from now? (Remember floppy disks? Zip disks? Probably not.) What is your plan for transferring your files to an upgraded storage device? Or do you anticipate a time when you will stop caring about the files altogether?

Many of these questions depend on what the project is, how important it is that you and other people continue to have access to it, and what its longevity (its usefulness and rhetorical purposefulness) is expected to be. We're not all famous people who need our every digital file archived in the Library of Congress, but that doesn't mean we should just randomly delete stuff. Depending on your career path, you might need to create a portfolio of your work or refer back to an example or use an old photo in a new project. Be judicious about deleting—it should be a decision that is directly tied to the rhetorical situation of your text, as well as to future, unknown rhetorical situations that are probable, given who you are and what you're likely to do with your life. Storage is cheap and getting cheaper all the time. Plus, you'll never know what you'll want to show your great-grandkids, nieces and nephews, friends, or cyborg pets in the future.

◉— Touchpoint: Creating a Sustainability Plan

Use the questions in this chapter to craft a sustainability plan for your project or the work you have done in your class so far this semester. Think about whether you might use this project in a future portfolio, build from it in a future project, or refer back to it in a workplace situation. This plan should include descriptions of where the project will reside (i.e., the storage and/or delivery medium), who will have access to it, what the access codes are (if any), and any other relevant information. In other words, how will your project endure after you've completed it? For most of these questions, there is no clear-cut answer. Instead, it is a matter of weighing the pros and cons to find the solution that is best for your project's particular rhetorical situation.

Index